W9-CEI-896

Tea-time Recipes

Tea-time Recipes

Jane Pettigrew

Special Photography by
Andreas von Einsiedel

 THE NATIONAL TRUST

First published in Great Britain in 1991 by
National Trust Enterprises Limited.
Reprinted 1992, 1993 and 1995.

Revised edition published in Great Britain in 2001 by
National Trust Enterprises Limited, 36 Queen Anne's Gate,
London SW1H 9AS

http://www.nationaltrust.org.uk/bookshop

British Library Cataloguing Publication Data
A Catalogue record for this book is available from the British Library

ISBN 0-7078-0287-3

Photographs: NTPL/Andreas von Einsiedel

Designed by Newton Engert Partnership

Phototypeset in Caslon by SPAN Graphics Limited

Printed and bound in Italy by G. Canale & C.s.p.A

Contents

Acknowledgements 6

Introduction 7

Successful Baking 11

Conversions 19

American Equivalents 20

The South-West 21

The South-East 54

Eastern Counties 71

Heart of England 83

The North-East 95

The North-West 109

Wales 123

Northern Ireland 132

National Trust Restaurants and Tea-rooms 143

Index 149

Acknowledgements

In the first edition of this book, I thanked the people who helped me with the history of the various National Trust properties and anecdotes about afternoon tea. I also acknowledged the cooks and chefs who gave me their recipes. I would like to thank them all again, as the information they provided has splendidly survived the passage of time: Norma Archer; Judith Beech; David Bentley; Maire Bermingham; Mary Berry; Joan Brown; Biddy Carson; Ann Chamberlain; Peter Cunninghame; Stella Curley; Ann Denford; Maureen Dodsworth; Kathleen Elliot; Doreen Gaynor; Jackie George; Sybil Gill; Fred Groves; Sue Hamby; Susan Hannaford; Mike Hemming; Diane Henry; Sue Hind; Simone Horn; Margaret Hughes; Gill Hunter; Jackie Ikin; Liz Ingram; Betty Jones; Rita Jones; Maureen Keen; Isabelle King; Jenny Kirk; Stuart Knight; Michelle Lewars; Jane Longhurst; Andrea Marchington; Dorothy Martin; Shelagh Matthews; Irene McAleese; Joyce McCready; Christine Milson; Elizabeth Murgatroyd; Neil O'Connor; Mary Parsons; Hazel Philips; Gill Pickering; Marian Randall; Suzanne Roberts; Jean Robinson; Shirley Santos; Wendy Scerri; Joan Sears; Joan Simons; Di Smallman; Edith Smith; Maureen Smith; Jayne Spencely; Anne Taylor; Tim Tebbs; Melanie Thomas; Sue Thompson; Karin Tucker; Barbara Twiss; Virginia Watergate; Ann West; Tam White; Hazel Williams; Ann Willoughby; Jane Wood.

For this new edition of the book, I would like to thank Andreas von Einsiedel and his assistant, Kevin Alderman, for their patience and skill in photographing the tea shots. These were taken at Saltram House in Devon in March 2000, shortly before the house re-opened to visitors. The staff at Saltram were not only busy preparing for the opening of the season, but extended enormous kindness and forebearance to the National Trust's Publisher, Margaret Willes, and myself during the shoot. My last thanks, therefore, are to Kevan Timms, the property manager, Sue Baumbach, the house steward, Felicity Blomeley and her conservation assistants, Jane Wood (again), the catering manager, and Andy Norman, the chef, who baked many of the cakes and biscuits for the photographs, and finally to Mary Brown, who made and iced the Christmas cake so beautifully.

Jane Pettigrew, April 2000

INTRODUCTION

In the early days of the National Trust, visitors to the properties were sometimes offered a cup of tea and a bun at the kitchen door or in some suitable corner of the house or garden. Nowadays, many properties provide morning coffee, lunches, afternoon teas and sometimes evening meals or special functions in prestigious and stylish restaurants. The food is always of a high standard, and in many areas local people make special trips just to have lunch or tea at their nearby National Trust house or garden.

By sitting down to enjoy a cup of tea and a sandwich or a piece of cake, National Trust visitors are perpetuating a ritual that has its origins in Britain in the mid-seventeenth century, when tea started to arrive via Holland and Portugal which had established trade routes to Japan and China a hundred years earlier. Merchants and aristocrats imported small amounts of China tea into Britain in the 1650s, but it was Charles II's marriage in 1662 to a Portuguese princess, Catharine of Braganza, that established tea drinking as an accepted practice. Catharine brought to London a large chest of tea as part of her dowry; she quickly introduced this to her friends at court, regular consignments were soon being ordered for the King and Queen, and tea drinking became a fashionable activity. Meanwhile enterprising merchants, keen to increase sales of this new commodity, engaged in elaborate advertising campaigns, and gradually the trend spread. Tea was served, and loose tea sold, in the coffee houses that had sprung up in London and some provincial towns in the 1650s, but the high tax levied by Charles II meant that it was very expensive and therefore out of the reach of the working classes. Ale and gin continued to be the standard drinks of the majority of the population until 1784, when the tax was reduced from 119 per cent to the 12.5 per cent (to 2½d. per lb) and tea overtook them in the popularity stakes. Had the tax remained, it is likely that the British would have ended up drinking coffee like the French and Germans.

In the first half of the eighteenth century a powerful campaign against the coffee houses, which had become bawdy dens of iniquity, succeeded in closing them down, and, in their place, the pleasure gardens at Vaux-hall, Chelsea, Marylebone, Islington, Bermondsey, Kentish Town and Kilburn provided family entertainment in London. The price of entry to these gardens sometimes included tea with bread and butter, the idea being that, after enjoying rides on the river, horse-riding, listening to music or wandering through beautifully tended gardens, the family could relax and take some refreshment together. Sadly, the gardens survived for only a short time; by 1850 most had closed, but not before the ritual of afternoon tea had been firmly established as part of the British way of life. It is said to have been 'invented' in the early nineteenth century by Anna, wife of the 7th Duke of Bedford. Breakfast in those days was taken at nine or ten o'clock in the morning, and dinner, which had previously been eaten at two or three o'clock in the afternoon, was not until eight or nine o'clock. By four o'clock the Duchess, and no doubt others too, felt a little peckish; she therefore asked her maid to serve some tea and light refreshment in her rooms. The Duchess was so pleased with this arrangement that she started inviting her friends to join her, and soon all of London's elegant society was sipping tea and gossiping all the while about people, places and events. With their tea they nibbled dainty sandwiches or neat slices of light sponge cake flavoured with candied orange or lemon peel, or caraway seeds. As the custom of taking tea became more popular, so the demand for tea ware grew, and the potteries, silversmiths and furniture makers produced a wide range of tea services, cake plates, teaspoons, knives, strainers, teapots and kettles, caddies, caddy spoons and tea tables.

In 1884 the activities of the manageress of the London Bridge branch of the Aerated Bread Company (the ABC) brought afternoon tea out of the elegant salons of the aristocracy and into the realm of everyday middle- and working-class people. This enterprising lady, who was in the habit of offering a cup of tea and a chat to her regular customers when they came in to buy their loaves of bread, persuaded her employers to allow her to create a public tea-room on the premises. Other companies quickly followed suit and soon every high street had its ABC, Express Dairy, Lyons' or Kardomah tea-room. By the 1920s going out to tea was a pastime enjoyed by people from all classes and walks of life. Children who grew up during the Edwardian period have fond memories of tea out with nanny, and most people remember their favourite tea-rooms with nostalgia and pleasure.

In the 'posher' hotels and restaurants, tea dances became the craze from about 1912 onwards. A demonstration of the dance, which originated in the back streets of Buenos Aires, was given first in Paris and then in London. Initially couples danced between the restaurant tables, but, as the idea caught on, a space was cleared in the middle of the floor. Soon tango teas and matinées were being held in most hotels and in half a dozen theatres around London. Books were written telling society hostesses how to organise tea dances, restaurants started tango clubs, and dance teachers, such as Victor Silvester, made their fortunes. One well-known teacher of the time – Miss Gladys Beattie Crozier – wrote in her book *The Tango and How to Dance It*: 'What could be pleasanter on a dull wintry afternoon, at 5 o'clock or so, when calls or shopping are over, than to drop into one of the cheery little Thé Dansant clubs, which have sprung up all over the West End during the last month or two, to take one's place at a tiny table . . . set forth with the prettiest of gold and white china, to enjoy a most elaborate and delicious tea served within a moment of one's arrival, while listening to an excellent string band playing delicious haunting airs . . .'

Sadly, the fashion for tea gradually dwindled, and the tea-shops were replaced by fast-food chains with their plastic tables and American food. In the mid-1980s, however, there was a revival of interest. Tea companies introduced new, exciting blends with exotic and enticing names – Rose Pouchong, Keemun, Yunnan – as well as scented teas and herbal tisanes; new tea-shops opened in unlikely places and quickly became popular; a rash of books about tea including tea-time recipes appeared on bookshop shelves; tea dances again became the rage, even in provincial hotels and village halls; and going out for afternoon tea is now very much back in fashion. The National Trust tea-rooms have carried on regardless through the years of change, but here too there is a difference. The tea-rooms are expanding, a wider variety of cakes is being baked, and the tea served is now specially packaged for the Trust.

If you have always been a faithful drinker of good old 'British' tea, it is well worth experimenting with some of the speciality brews and blends. The delicate green, unfermented teas need no milk and have an extremely refreshing quality as well as a low caffeine content; the oolongs or pouchongs are halfway between green tea and black (fermented) tea; Lapsang Souchong from China has a delicious smoky flavour; Earl Grey is scented with citrus oil of bergamot; pure Darjeeling from the foothills of the Himalayas is often called the champagne of teas and has a delicate muscatel aroma; Kenya gives a full-bodied brisk taste; and Assam has a strong, malty flavour that is very good in the mornings.

Although tea is drunk and enjoyed throughout the day, the favourite time for many people is at four or five o'clock in the afternoon, when the refreshing cuppa is often accompanied by a sweet or savoury treat. This book offers a wide selection of breads, scones, cakes and biscuits served in National Trust tea-rooms and restaurants in England, Wales and Northern Ireland, as well as some traditional regional specialities. All are suitable fare for those who, in Samuel Johnson's words, may be 'a hardened and shameless tea-drinker, who has for twenty years diluted his meals with only the infusion of this fascinating plant; whose kettle has scarcely time to cool; who with tea amuses the evening, with tea solaces the midnight, and with tea welcomes the morning.'

SUCCESSFUL BAKING

Ingredients

FLOUR

PLAIN FLOUR is generally used when little rise is required; for example, pastries and shortbreads. To convert plain flour to self-raising flour, add baking powder in the quantities recommended on the container for different types of baking.

SELF-RAISING FLOUR is used for cakes which need a raising agent. In some recipes, however, the amount of raising agent already added to the flour may be too great; a mixture of plain and self-raising flour is therefore used.

Always store flour in a cool, dry place, preferably in an airtight container. Sift before use to remove any lumps and also to incorporate extra air before adding to the cake mixture.

RAISING AGENTS

BAKING POWDER is the most commonly used raising agent. It gives off carbon dioxide which forms bubbles in the mixture. These expand during cooking, making the cake, scone or biscuit rise and helping to produce a light texture. Too much baking powder can cause sogginess and heaviness.

BICARBONATE OF SODA is often used in recipes which include sour milk or buttermilk, spices, treacle and honey.

SOUR MILK is sometimes necessary to give extra rise to heavy mixtures, such as gingerbreads. It can be made at home by allowing milk to sit in a warm atmosphere until it curdles.

BUTTERMILK is a standard ingredient in Welsh and Irish cookery and is available in some supermarkets and from some milk-delivery companies.

YEAST was once the only raising agent available for home baking, but is now generally used only in breadmaking and in some traditional fruit or spice breads or pastries, such as saffron loaves, Chelsea buns and lardy cake. Dried yeast keeps for several months in an airtight container. Fresh yeast lasts for about a week in the refrigerator and will freeze for up to six months.

FATS

BUTTER AND MARGARINE are interchangeable in most recipes, but butter is preferable in shortbreads and rich fruit cakes, such as Christmas cake, that are to be stored and matured.

LARD is often used in biscuits and gives a shorter texture.

OIL is excellent in carrot cakes and chocolate cakes, and is ideal for anybody with a cholesterol problem.

Allow butter, margarine or lard to soften to room temperature for at least an hour before using. Soft or whipped margarines can be used straight from the refrigerator.

EGGS

EGGS should be at room temperature, as taken straight from the refrigerator they are more likely to curdle. Small eggs (sizes 5 and 6) are too small for most recipes. Use large (sizes 1 and 2) or medium (sizes 3 and 4).

SUGAR

CASTER SUGAR is generally used for creamed mixtures as it gives a much lighter texture.

GRANULATED SUGAR is acceptable in rubbed-in mixtures, but can produce a slightly gritty texture. It is worth paying a little extra for caster sugar.

DEMERARA SUGAR is very good in tea breads and in mixtures where ingredients are melted together, such as gingerbreads and boiled fruit cakes. It is excellent for sprinkling on the top of loaves and biscuits.

SOFT BROWN SUGAR gives a caramel flavour and beats well in creamed mixtures. The darker variety has a stronger flavour.

BLACK TREACLE has a dark colour and strong flavour and is often used in gingerbreads and some fruit cakes.

GOLDEN SYRUP gives a soft, moist, sometimes sticky texture which is suitable for gingerbreads and flapjacks.

HONEY adds a very special flavour but too much will cause the mixture to burn easily.

Preparing tins

Most non-stick cake tins are very reliable if you follow the manufacturers' instructions, but, to be on the safe side, it is wise to line and grease them anyway. Grease tins with whatever fat or oil is to be used in the recipe, then line with non-stick greaseproof parchment. Cut a single piece for the bottom of the tin and, when fitting paper to the sides, cut into the corners to make quite sure that it lies neatly against the tin. It may also be necessary to cut and overlap the paper, as the sides of circular tins sometimes slope slightly.

Oven temperatures

Always make sure that the oven has reached the correct temperature before putting in the item to be baked. If you are not sure whether your oven is accurate, buy an oven thermometer and make regular checks. If using a convection oven, reduce all recommended temperatures by 20°C.

Cakes, scones and biscuits

Always use the right tin for the recipe. Smaller or larger tins will affect the cooking time and hence the texture of the finished cake or biscuits.

Except in fan-assisted ovens, most cakes and biscuits cook best in the middle of the oven. Rich fruit cakes, large cakes and shortbreads should be placed just below the centre, and small, plain cakes, Swiss rolls and scones just above.

Do not disturb the cake during the first three-quarters of the baking time and, better still, not until you think it may be ready. Draughts and knocks can make the cake sink.

When placing biscuits on prepared tins, always allow room for them to spread during baking. It is better to leave too much room than to have all the biscuits merging into one misshapen mass.

Is it ready?

To see if a sponge cake is ready, press lightly with a finger; if it springs back it is cooked. To test fruit cakes and gingerbreads, stick a skewer into the middle of the cake and withdraw it immediately. If the skewer comes out clean, the cake is done. If not, allow a further 15 minutes and test again. Biscuits are usually ready when they are just turning golden. Scones are firm, well risen and golden when cooked.

If a cake begins to darken too quickly, place a double or triple layer of greaseproof paper over the top and continue cooking as usual.

Pastry

The aim is to make pastry as light as possible, and this depends on how much cold air is trapped in the mixture before baking. The secret is to use cold ingredients, to have cold hands, cold bowls, a cold slab or surface on which to roll (marble is ideal) and work in a cool room. Work quickly and lightly, using the fingertips when rubbing in, as too much handling makes the pastry tough. When rolling, sprinkle only a little flour on to the work surface and use light, even movements.

Most pastry recipes call for plain flour, but self-raising is sometimes used for suet crust and shortcrust. The more fat is used, the shorter the pastry will be; if the amount of fat is less than half the amount of flour, add 1 teaspoon of baking powder for each 8oz (225g) of flour. Butter, or butter mixed with lard, is best.

Rich pastry needs a hotter oven than others. If the oven is too cool, the fat will run out of the pastry and the pastry will be tough and chewy.

LINING PIE DISHES
AND PLATES

Roll out the pastry to a thickness of about ⅛–¼in (0·25–0·5cm) and a little larger in size than the prepared dish or plate. Lay the pastry carefully on the dish, making sure that no air is trapped underneath. Do not stretch the pastry as it will only shrink back. If it is not big enough, roll out a little more and try again. Ease the pastry into all the rims and corners of the dish, then trim off any surplus. (Trimmings may be useful to make crosses on hot cross buns or a trellis over the top of a tart or pie.)

BAKING BLIND

This is necessary when an uncooked filling is to be put into the pastry case, or to set the pastry before any filling is poured in and cooked. When the prepared tin has been greased and lined with the pastry, prick the base all over with a fork. Cover the base with a piece of greaseproof paper followed by a layer of metal baking beans (available in any good cookware shop) or pasta or pulses (dried haricot beans, dried kidney beans or chickpeas). Bake in a preheated oven for just under the required time, then remove from the oven, lift out the baking beans and the greaseproof paper and bake for 5 minutes more to dry out the base.

Pastry recipes

FLAKY PASTRY

1lb (450g) plain flour, sifted
teaspoon salt
12oz (350g) butter, or half butter
  and half lard, softened

1 teaspoon lemon juice
10fl oz (300ml) cold water

Mix together the flour and salt. Divide the fat into four portions. Rub one portion into the flour with the fingertips. Mix in the lemon juice and cold water to give a soft dough, rather like the consistency of butter. Knead gently on a lightly floured board until smooth. Roll out to a rectangle three times longer than it is wide. Dot the second portion of fat over the top two-thirds of the surface. Fold up the bottom third and fold down the top third and seal the edges by pressing together with a rolling pin. Wrap in cling film or a plastic bag and chill for 15 minutes. Place the dough on the floured board with the folded edges to your right and left, and roll out again to a rectangle. Repeat the dotting, folding and chilling process twice more until all the fat is used. Wrap again and chill for at least 45 minutes before using.

PUFF PASTRY

1lb (450g) plain flour, sifted
1 teaspoon salt
1lb (450g) butter, softened

1 teaspoon lemon juice
3–4fl oz (75–100ml) iced water

Mix together the flour and salt. Add 2oz (50g) of the butter, cut into small pieces, and rub into the flour until the mixture resembles fine breadcrumbs. Add the lemon juice and enough water to give a soft dough, similar to the consistency of butter. Knead lightly until really smooth. In a clean linen cloth, shape the remaining butter into a rectangle. On a lightly floured board, roll out the pastry to a rectangle slightly wider than the rectangle of butter and about twice its length. Place the butter on one half of the pastry and fold the other half over. Press the edges together with a rolling pin. Leave in a cool place for 15 minutes to allow the butter to harden slightly. Roll out the pastry to a long strip three times its original length, but keeping the width the same. The corners should be square, the sides straight and the thickness even. The butter must not break through the dough. Fold the bottom third up and the top third down, press the edges together with a rolling pin, put inside a well-oiled plastic bag and chill for 30 minutes. Place the dough on the floured board with the folded edges to your right and left, and roll out into a long strip as before. Fold again into three and chill for a further

30 minutes. Repeat this process four times more and chill for 30 minutes before using.

This is best made over two days, rolling three times and chilling overnight before completing the rolling the following day.

| RICH SHORTCRUST PASTRY | *1lb (450g) plain flour, sifted*
a good pinch of salt
12oz (350g) butter, softened | *2 egg yolks*
4 teaspoons caster sugar
3–4 tablespoons cold water |

Mix together the flour and salt. Rub in the butter until the mixture resembles breadcrumbs. Make a well in the middle, add the egg yolks and sugar and mix with a round-bladed knife. Add enough of the water, a little at a time, to give a stiff but pliable dough. Knead lightly until smooth. Wrap in cling film or a plastic bag and chill for at least 15 minutes before using.

| ROUGH PUFF PASTRY | *1lb (450g) plain flour, sifted*
a pinch of salt
12oz (350g) butter, or half butter
  and half lard, softened | *1 teaspoon lemon juice*
3–4 tablespoons cold water |

Mix together the flour and salt. Cut the fat into small pieces and stir lightly into the flour with a round-bladed knife. Make a well in the middle, add the lemon juice and mix with enough water to give an elastic dough. On a lightly floured board, roll out the dough to a long strip, keeping the sides straight and the corners square. Fold up the bottom third and fold down the top third and turn the dough so that the folded edges are to your right and left. Repeat the rolling and folding process three times more, chilling the pastry for 15 minutes between the third and fourth rolling. Chill for at least 15 minutes before using.

| SHORTCRUST PASTRY | *1lb (450g) plain flour, sifted*
a pinch of salt
4oz (100g) margarine or butter,
  softened | *4oz (100g) lard, softened*
3–4 tablespoons cold water |

Mix together the flour and salt. Cut the fats into small pieces and rub into the flour until the mixture resembles fine breadcrumbs. Gradually add enough water, mixing with a fork, to give a stiff but pliable dough. Knead lightly for a few minutes until smooth. Wrap in cling film or a plastic bag and chill for at least 15 minutes before using.

Bread

The most commonly used flour for breadmaking is wheat. Strong wheat flour has a high gluten content and gives a better volume of bread, as it absorbs more water and makes a lighter dough. White flour is made from the starchy part of the grain from which the fibre and wheatgerm has been removed. Wholewheat flour is made from 100 per cent of the grain; nothing is added and nothing is taken away. Wheatmeal is made from 81–85 per cent of the grain and some of the fibre and wheatgerm has been removed.

Bread can be made with a variety of other grains. Rye gives a dark dough and is usually mixed half and half with wheat flour; barley gives a cake-like texture and is usually mixed with wheat flour; maize gives a crumbly, crunchy texture. Other ingredients can be added to achieve different results; for example, extra bran, wheatgerm, sesame, poppy or sunflower seeds, cheese, herbs, spices, lemon or orange rind and rye flakes.

KNEADING

Kneading is an essential part of breadmaking as it helps to develop the gluten and the rise of the dough. Flour a board and use the palms of the hands, almost to the wrists, to push and turn the dough. As you work you can actually feel the texture changing to a smooth, elastic but not sticky consistency.

PROVING

Always cover the dough when setting it to prove; any draughts may affect the process. The yeast in the dough needs warmth to start working; the ideal temperature is between 98 and 110°F (36 and 44°C). Too much heat will kill the yeast; too little will stop it from working. The best place to leave dough to prove is on top of an Aga, a boiler or an active tumble dryer. The time taken for the dough to rise will depend on the warmth, but it usually takes 1–1½ hours. The second rising is quicker, usually between 20 minutes and half an hour.

Possible failures and solutions

FRUIT CAKES

If the fruit sinks to the bottom of the cake, it is probably because there was too little beating of fat and sugar, too much liquid or too much raising agent.

If the cake sinks in the middle, it may be because the oven was not hot enough, or there was too little creaming of fat and sugar, or there was too much raising agent.

If the cake is dry, it is usually because there was not enough liquid, or it is overcooked.

If the top of the cake is cracked, the tin was too small and the oven was too hot.

SANDWICH AND
SPONGE CAKES

If the outside is too dark and the inside is not properly cooked, the oven was too hot and the cake was too near the top.

If the top of the cake is domed, the oven was too hot or there was not enough beating.

If the sponge does not rise well, there was too little raising agent or the oven was too cool.

SCONES

If the scones are tough, there was probably too much kneading.

If the scones are hard and not spongy, there was too little liquid.

If the scones are soggy in the middle, the oven was too cool or they were too low in the oven.

If the scones have not risen, there was too little raising agent.

YEASTED BREADS
AND CAKES

If the cake or loaf is smaller than expected, there was either too much or too little raising agent, or the yeast did not activate properly due to incorrect temperature during proving.

If the texture of the cake or loaf is coarse, the yeast was not properly mixed at the beginning, or there was too much yeast which caused excessive rising and air in the dough.

Conversions

The following approximate conversions are used throughout this book. Use a standard teacup for measuring.

½ oz	15 g	¼ in	0·5 cm	
1 oz	25 g	½ in	1 cm	
2 oz	50 g	¾ in	1·5 cm	
3 oz	75 g	1 in	2·5 cm	
4 oz	100 g	2 in	5 cm	
5 oz	150 g	3 in	7·5 cm	
6 oz	175 g	4 in	10 cm	
7 oz	200 g	5 in	12·5 cm	
8 oz	225 g	6 in	15 cm	
9 oz	250 g	7 in	17·5 cm	
10 oz	275 g	8 in	20 cm	
11 oz	300 g	9 in	22·5 cm	
12 oz	350 g	10 in	25 cm	
13 oz	375 g	11 in	27·5 cm	
14 oz	400 g	12 in	30 cm	
15 oz	425 g			
1 lb	450 g			
1½ lb	675 g			
2 lb	900 g	gas mark ¼	225°F	110°C
		gas mark ½	250°F	120°C
1 fl oz	25 ml	gas mark 1	275°F	140°C
2 fl oz	50 ml	gas mark 2	300°F	150°C
3 fl oz	75 ml	gas mark 3	325°F	160°C
4 fl oz	100 ml	gas mark 4	350°F	180°C
5 fl oz (¼ pint)	150 ml	gas mark 5	375°F	190°C
10 fl oz (½ pint)	300 ml	gas mark 6	400°F	200°C
12 fl oz	350 ml	gas mark 7	425°F	220°C
15 fl oz	400 ml	gas mark 8	450°F	230°C
20 fl oz (1 pint)	600 ml	gas mark 9	475°F	240°C

American Equivalents

DRY MEASURES

1 US cup	=	50 g	=	2 oz	breadcrumbs; cake crumbs

1 US cup = 50 g = 2 oz breadcrumbs; cake crumbs

1 US cup = 75 g = 3 oz porridge or rolled oats

1 US cup = 90 g = 3½ oz ground almonds; shredded coconut

1 US cup = 100 g = 4 oz roughly chopped walnuts and other nuts; icing sugar; cocoa; drinking chocolate; flaked almonds; grated Cheddar cheese

1 US cup = 150 g = 5 oz white flour; currants; rice flour; muesli; cornflour; chopped dates

1 US cup = 175 g = 6 oz wholemeal flour; oatmeal; raisins; sultanas; dried apricots; mixed candied peel

1 US cup = 200 g = 7 oz caster sugar; soft brown sugar; demerara sugar; rice; glacé cherries; semolina; chopped figs or plums

1 US cup = 225 g = 8 oz granulated sugar; curd cheese; cream cheese

1 US cup = 300 g = 11 oz mincemeat; marmalade; jam

1 US cup = 350 g = 12 oz golden syrup; black treacle

LIQUID MEASURES

⅛ US cup = 25 ml = 1 fl oz

¼ US cup = 50 ml = 2 fl oz

½ US cup = 100 ml = 4 fl oz

1 US cup = 225 ml = 8 fl oz

1¼ US cups = 300 ml = 10 fl oz

1¾ US cups = 400 ml = 15 fl oz

2 US cups = 475 ml = 16 fl oz

2½ US cups = 600 ml = 20 fl oz

MEASURES FOR FATS

¼ stick = 25 g = 2 level tablespoons = 1 oz

1 stick (½ US cup) = 100 g = 8 level tablespoons = 4 oz

The South-West

Cornwall and Devon are famous for their cream teas, served with clotted cream. The Devon variety is thicker and more buttery because of the lush pasture on which the cows graze, whereas Cornish clotted cream tends to be whiter and lighter. The cream is made by leaving rich creamy milk to stand for twenty-four hours in winter and twelve hours in summer; the milk is then gently heated until small rings and undulations appear on the surface. The liquid is set in a cool place and left until the following day when the clotted cream is carefully skimmed off. Cream teas are normally served in Cornwall with Cornish splits – the soft white yeast buns that are more common than scones in the duchy.

Spices have been widely used in cookery in the south west since the days of early trading with the Orient, when they arrived by ship in the ports of Cornwall and Devon and were therefore readily available. As a result, there are cakes baked with ginger, cinnamon, nutmeg and saffron, believed to have medicinal qualities but also popular as a flavouring and colouring in medieval dishes. Saffron cakes and buns are traditional fare for festive occasions, particularly Lent, at Easter and annual fairs. Indeed, saffron cakes are more common in Cornwall than in Essex, where vast estates of blue crocuses produced home-grown saffron in the fourteenth century. Ships from the West Indies also sought haven in the ports of the south west; Chocolate Rum Cake from St Michael's Mount recalls this trade.

Hampshire is noted for its strawberries, which make an excellent filling for shortcakes, sponges and flans. Further west, the apple is king, widely used in deliciously moist cakes.

From Bath come Sally Lunns – soft, slightly sweet tea cakes which are said to be named after the street vendor who sold them in the eighteenth century. According to another story, however, the name derives from the French, *soleil lune*, so called because the tops were golden and round like the sun and the bottoms were pale and flat like the moon. Other early spellings were Soli Lume, Sollylum and Solemena. Whatever the origins of the name, it is customary to split the freshly baked, warm cake, and fill it with cream rather than butter. Bath buns were another traditional treat. In the early eighteenth century they were flavoured with sherry, rose water and carraway seeds, but the modern version contains candied peel and currants, and is topped with the characteristic crushed lump sugar which gives the buns their distinctive crunchy quality.

BEDRUTHAN STEPS

Bedruthan became a popular venue for carriage drives from Newquay when the town was developed as a holiday resort in the 1880s. The famous view of yellow sands and a sparkling blue sea on a fine summer's day must have appeared on more postcards than anywhere else in Cornwall, yet in winter it can be an awesome sight in a force ten gale.

The name Bedruthan Steps was first recorded in 1851 and appears to refer to the precipitous cliff staircase which leads down to the south end of the beach. (Unfortunately, the Trust was forced to close the staircase in 1990 because of the danger to visitors from the friable rock face.) The name has since been applied to the several isolated stacks along the beach, the hard rock still standing after the softer rock surrounding it has been eroded away.

Apricot Swiss Roll

Serves 6

FOR THE SPONGE
2 eggs
3oz (75g) caster sugar
3oz (75g) self-raising flour, sifted

FOR THE FILLING
1 × 14½ oz (410g) tin apricots,
    drained and the juice reserved
1–2 tablespoons brandy
5fl oz (150ml) whipped cream
1oz (25g) flaked almonds, untoasted
1oz (25g) flaked almonds, toasted
icing sugar for dusting

To make the sponge, preheat the oven to gas mark 3/325°F/160°C. Grease and line a 7 × 11in (17·5 × 27·5cm) tin. Beat the eggs thoroughly. Add the sugar and continue beating until frothy. Fold in the flour and turn into the prepared tin. Bake for 10-15 minutes until the sponge springs back when lightly pressed. Remove from the oven and invert the tin on to a clean tea-cloth dusted with a little caster sugar. Roll the sponge immediately round a wooden rolling pin or a milk bottle and leave to cool. Meanwhile slice the apricots and soak in the brandy. Just before serving, carefully unroll the sponge and spread with the whipped cream. Arrange the apricots over the top and pour on the brandy. Sprinkle with the untoasted almonds and carefully roll the sponge up again. Place on a serving dish, pour a little of the reserved apricot juice over the sponge, sprinkle the top with toasted almonds and dust with icing sugar. Serve immediately.

This makes a mouthwatering dessert or a very special cake for tea.

Eggless Scones

Makes approximately
12 scones

12oz (350g) self-raising flour, sifted
2oz (50g) margarine, softened

2oz (50g) lard, softened
4-4½ fl oz (100-115ml) milk

Preheat the oven to gas mark 5/375°F/190°C. Grease two baking trays. Rub the fats into the flour, working as quickly and lightly as possible with cold hands. Add enough milk to give a soft, bread-like dough. On a floured board, roll out to a thickness of ¾in (1·5cm) and cut into rounds with a 2½in (6cm) cutter. Place on the prepared trays and bake for 15-20 minutes until lightly golden and well risen. Remove from the oven and lift on to a wire rack to cool.

Despite containing no eggs, this recipe makes light, well-risen scones that are perfect served warm with jam and Cornish clotted cream.

BRANSCOMBE BAKERY

The bakehouse at Branscombe, the last traditional bakery to operate in Devon, continued to be run until 1987 by two brothers, Gerald and Stuart Collier (and by their father before them), along the lines set up many years earlier. The oven, fuelled by faggots, was lit every morning at four o'clock, and three and a half hours later, when the oven was hot enough, the ashes were raked out and the oven cleaned before the first batch of 130 loaves was baked. A second batch included more bread, cakes, buns, jam tarts and scones. On cold days the bread dough was set to rise in the special proving oven underneath the baking oven.

Organic Wholewheat Bread

Makes 2 × 2lb (900g)
loaves

1oz (25g) fresh yeast
½ teaspoon light or dark soft brown sugar
1-1¼ pints (600-750ml) warm water (it should be almost hand-hot, and the amount needed varies according to the flour used)

2lb (900g) organic wholemeal flour, sifted and warmed slightly in the oven
1 tablespoon sea salt
1 tablespoon corn or sunflower oil
1 tablespoon clear honey

Cream together the yeast and sugar and blend with 2-3fl oz (50-75ml) of the warm water. Leave in a warm, draught-free place for 10-20 minutes until frothy (there should be at least ¾in (1·5cm) of froth on the top). Mix together the flour and salt and make a well in the middle. Pour in the oil, honey, yeast mixture and enough of the remaining water to give a soft, elastic dough. Knead with the hands for about 10 minutes. Shape the dough into a ball and place in a lightly greased bowl. Dust the top with a little flour, cover with a clean damp cloth and leave in a warm, draught-free place until almost doubled in size (this can take anything from 50 minutes to 2 hours). Grease two 2lb (900g) loaf tins. Turn the dough out on to a lightly floured board and knead vigorously for 8–10 minutes. Divide the dough into two equal portions and shape to fit the tins. Place in the tins, sprinkle the tops with a little more flour and cover with a clean damp cloth. Leave in a warm place for a further 30–40 minutes until the dough reaches the top of the tins. Meanwhile heat the oven to gas mark 7/425°F/220°C. When the dough has risen, bake the loaves for 30 minutes. Remove from the oven and remove from the tins. Place the loaves in the oven for a further 10–15 minutes until they sound hollow when tapped. Remove from the oven and cool on a wire rack.

Sunday-Best Chocolate Cake

Makes 1 × 8in (20cm) 3-tier cake

FOR THE CAKE

8oz (225g) plain wholemeal flour, sifted
5 level teaspoons baking powder
8oz (225g) margarine, softened

8oz (225g) light or dark soft brown sugar
5 large eggs, beaten
3 tablespoons cocoa powder, sifted

FOR THE FILLING AND TOPPING
12fl oz (350ml) single cream
24oz (675g) white chocolate, grated

Preheat the oven to gas mark 3/325°F/160°C. Grease and line three 8in (20cm) round sandwich tins. Place all the ingredients for the cake in a large bowl and beat thoroughly to give a soft, dropping consistency (add a little water if too dry). Divide equally between the prepared tins and smooth the tops. Bake for about 30 minutes until the sponge springs back when lightly pressed. Remove from the oven and turn out on to a wire rack to cool. Next make the filling and topping. Bring the cream just to boiling point in a heavy pan and stir in the chocolate. Remove from the heat and stir until well blended. Leave in a cool place until it has achieved the right consistency for spreading. Use to sandwich the cakes together and to cover the top. Decorate with grated dark chocolate, fat curls of white chocolate or chocolate buttons.

This makes a spectacular gâteau which is suitable for birthday parties or as a dinner-party dessert.

An Easter Tea, clockwise from the top: Derbyshire spiced fruit bread (page 94); Simnel cake (page 30); hot cross buns (page 47); Easter biscuits (page 41).

Wholemeal Cider Cake

Makes 1 × 2lb (900g) loaf

4oz (100g) sultanas
3oz (75g) currants
1oz (25g) mixed candied peel
5fl oz (150ml) cider
5oz (150g) self-raising wholemeal
    flour, sifted
3oz (75g) dark soft brown sugar

2oz (50g) hazelnuts or blanched
    almonds, chopped
the finely grated rind of 1 lemon
the finely grated rind of 1 orange
1 eating apple, peeled, cored and
    chopped
2 medium eggs, beaten

Put the dried fruit and the cider into a pan and bring to the boil. Remove from the heat and leave to stand overnight. The following day preheat the oven to gas mark 4/350°F/180°C. Grease and line a 2lb (900g) loaf tin. Mix together the flour, sugar, nuts, orange and lemon peel, apple and beaten eggs and pour in the cider mixture. Beat thoroughly, then turn into the prepared tin. Bake for about 1 hour until a skewer comes out clean. Remove from the oven and turn out on to a wire rack to cool.

BUCKLAND ABBEY

Set among sloping green lawns and exotic trees and shrubs on the edge of the sleepy Tavy Valley, Buckland Abbey is rich in associations with Francis Drake and in echoes of the great Cistercian monastery it once was. A national hero on his return from circumnavigating the world in 1580, Drake needed a house which reflected his newly acquired status, ironically choosing to purchase the abbey which had been recently converted by his rival, Sir Richard Grenville.

Imaginative displays in the long gallery running the length of the top floor outline the history of the abbey from medieval times to the present day. Mementoes of Drake on the floor below include Elizabeth I's commission of 5 March 1587, giving Drake command of the fleet with which he 'singed the King of Spain's beard'. The only complete interior surviving from these times is the fine sixteenth-century great hall; a Georgian dining-room and the elegant staircase were added during late eighteenth-century improvements. On the ground floor the old kitchen of 1576 has two vast ranges with spits and ovens, and an attractive display of copper pots and pans, pewter tankards and stone jelly moulds, as well as some very pretty china.

A Cornish Tea, clockwise from the top: black cake (page 52); Cornish splits (page 37); saffron cake (page 30); Cornish fairings (page 40).

Chocolate Truffle Cake

Makes 9 pieces

1½ lb (675g) left-over cake (any sort), broken into small pieces
4oz (100g) jam (any sort)
2oz (50g) mixed, unsalted nuts, roughly chopped
2oz (50g) cocoa powder, sifted

3–4 tablespoons orange juice
8–10oz (225-275g) milk or plain chocolate
2oz (50g) blanched, split almonds, toasted

Grease and line a 7in (17·5cm) square tin. Mix together the cake, jam, nuts, cocoa powder and enough juice to bind the mixture. Press into the prepared tin and smooth the top. Melt the chocolate and pour over the surface. Spread evenly and sprinkle with the almonds. Place in the refrigerator to set. When set, cut into pieces and lift carefully out of the tin.

This is an excellent and quick way to turn left-over cake into a rich, delicious chocolate treat.

Date and Apple Slice

Makes 10–12 slices

1lb (450g) Coxes eating apples, with the peel left on, cored and diced
3oz (75g) mixed, unsalted nuts, roughly chopped
4oz (100g) stoned dates, roughly chopped

4oz (100g) self-raising flour, sifted
4oz (100g) dark soft brown or demerara sugar
1 tablespoon clear honey
1oz (25g) butter, melted
1 egg, beaten
a pinch of salt

Preheat the oven to gas mark 6/400°F/200°C. Grease a 7 × 11in (17·5 × 27·5cm) Swiss roll tin. Mix all the ingredients together and beat with a wooden spoon to ensure that they are evenly distributed. Turn into the prepared tin and press flat. Bake for 30 minutes until firm and golden. Remove from the oven and leave to cool in the tin. When cold, cut into slices and lift carefully from the tin.

'Take some more tea,' the March Hare said to Alice, very earnestly. 'I've had nothing yet,' Alice replied in an offended tone, 'so I can't take more.'

Lewis Carroll (1832-98), *Alice's Adventures in Wonderland*

Sherry Fruit Cake

Makes 1 × 8in (20cm) round cake

9oz (250g) mixed dried fruit
6oz (175g) glacé cherries, halved
6–7fl oz (175–200ml) sweet sherry
8oz (225g) butter, softened
8oz (225g) light soft brown sugar

3 eggs, beaten
8oz (225g) plain wholemeal flour, sifted
1 teaspoon baking powder

Soak the dried fruit and the cherries in the sherry overnight. The next day, preheat the oven to gas mark 3/325°F/160°C. Grease and line an 8in (20cm) round tin. Beat together the butter and sugar until light and fluffy. Gradually add the beaten eggs and beat hard. Mix together the flour and baking powder and fold into the mixture. Add the soaked fruit and sherry and mix well so that all the ingredients are evenly distributed. Turn into the prepared tin and bake for 1¾-2 hours until a skewer comes out clean. Remove from the oven and leave to cool in the tin for about 15 minutes before turning out on to a wire rack to cool completely.

CASTLE DROGO

Castle Drogo dominates a craggy hilltop that faces west over Dartmoor. This imposing fortress was commissioned in 1900 from Sir Edwin Lutyens, then at the height of his powers. It was built with the wealth amassed by the self-made millionaire Julius Drewe from his successful Home and Colonial Stores which he set up with a partner in 1883. His grandfather was a London tea merchant, and his mother's brother a tea importer. His first job was as a tea buyer in the Far East, but in 1878 he opened his own shop, The Willow Pattern Tea Store, in Liverpool. He was responsible for buying mainly Indian tea and he played a major part in converting the British from China to Indian blends. In 1833 the East India Company lost its monopoly on the tea trade with China and looked elsewhere to establish tea plantations. Upper Assam in India proved to be an ideal growing area and the first Indian tea arrived in Britain in November 1838. Ceylon did not enter the market until 1875.

Inside the mock-medieval structure of Castle Drogo Lutyens had designed a comfortable family home. Tea was always served in the library; this was a 'wonderful meal with wafer-thin bread and butter, scones and jam and Devonshire cream – and cakes in great variety followed by whatever fruit was in season'. Sadly, Julius Drewe died only a year after the castle was completed in 1930, but he must have been pleased with his progress in life. Whereas his similarly wealthy retailing rivals Lipton and Sainsbury were ignored by Burke's *Landed Gentry*, the acres he acquired with his fortune gained his inclusion.

Cider Loaf

Makes 1 × 2lb (900g) loaf

FOR THE LOAF
12oz (350g) self-raising flour, sifted
1 teaspoon mixed spice
8oz (225g) raisins
4oz (100g) butter
4oz (100g) light soft brown sugar
5fl oz (150ml) milk
5fl oz (150ml) dry cider
1 large egg, beaten
the grated rind of 1 orange

FOR THE ICING
4oz (100g) icing sugar
1-2 teaspoons orange juice
1-2 teaspoons cider

Preheat the oven to gas mark 4/350°F/180°C. Grease and line a 2lb (900g) loaf tin. Mix together the flour and spice and add the raisins. Melt the butter and add the sugar. Mix the milk with the cider (it will curdle, but do not worry) and stir into the flour with the butter and sugar mixture, the egg and orange rind. Mix well, then turn into the prepared tin and bake for 30 minutes. Reduce the oven temperature to gas mark 3/325°F/160°C and bake for a further 45 minutes until a skewer comes out clean. Remove from the oven and turn out on to a wire rack to cool. When cold, mix together the icing sugar, orange juice and cider to make a spreadable but not too runny icing and pour over the top of the cake.

The restaurant at Montacute House in Somerset serves a similar cake which is topped with an icing made with 2-3 teaspoons clear honey and 3-4oz (75-100g) icing sugar. This makes a delicious alternative to the cider topping.

Sticky Lemon Cake

Makes 1 × 7in (17·5cm) round cake

FOR THE CAKE
4oz (100g) margarine, softened
4oz (100g) caster sugar
2 eggs
4oz (100g) self-raising flour, sifted
the grated rind of half a lemon
the juice of half a lemon
1½ tablespoons icing sugar, sifted

FOR THE ICING
2-3oz (50-75g) icing sugar, sifted
the juice and finely grated rind of half a lemon

Preheat the oven to gas mark 3/325°F/160°C. Grease and line a 7in (17·5cm) round tin. Beat together the margarine and sugar until light and fluffy. Beat in the eggs, one at a time, whisking hard after the addition of each one. Fold in the flour and rind, mix well and turn into the prepared tin. Bake for 45 minutes until a skewer comes out clean. Remove from the oven and make several holes in the top of the cake with a skewer. Mix together the icing sugar and lemon juice and pour over the cake. Leave in the tin until absolutely cold. Meanwhile make the icing. Mix together the icing sugar, lemon rind and juice. When the cake is cold, turn out and ice with the prepared mixture.

COTEHELE

Cotehele is a medieval courtyard house set in beautiful grounds above the River Tamar, which for centuries was the only effective route to the outside world. The approach, the arch of the gateway just wide enough to admit a loaded packhorse, signals the character of the house, left virtually undisturbed for over 200 years from the end of the seventeenth century, when the Edgcumbe family chose to live at their grander seat overlooking Plymouth Sound.

Cotehele rambles in unexpected directions and on unusual levels, and is filled with many of its original furnishings and artefacts. The immense oven in the north wall of the kitchen is of particular interest, more than seven feet across and three feet high, with a smaller baking oven beside it. An oven of this size would have been essential to meet the demands of a large Tudor household. The kitchen contains many other gadgets and cooking utensils which tell a fascinating story about food and food preparation in the sixteenth and seventeenth centuries. A domed dove-cote and a stewpond near the house provided meat and fish for what was largely a self-sufficient community.

Boiled Date and Walnut Loaf

Makes 1 × 2lb (900g) loaf

8oz (225g) self-raising flour, sifted
2oz (50g) whole walnuts
1 teaspoon mixed spice
3oz (75g) margarine, softened
4oz (100g) light or dark soft
  brown sugar
8oz (225g) whole dates
5fl oz (150ml) water
2 eggs, beaten
2 tablespoons sesame seeds

Preheat the oven to gas mark 4/350°F/180°C. Grease and line a 2lb (900g) loaf tin. Mix together the flour, walnuts and mixed spice. Place the margarine, sugar, dates and water in a pan and bring gently to the boil. Remove from the heat and cool for a few minutes. Add to the flour, spice and nuts with the beaten eggs and beat well. Turn into the prepared tin, hollow the middle a little and sprinkle the top with the sesame seeds. Bake for 1–1¼ hours until a skewer comes out clean. Remove from the oven and turn out on to a wire rack to cool. Serve sliced with butter.

Saffron Cake

Makes 1 × 2lb (900g) loaf

½ oz (15g) fresh yeast
1¼ oz (32g) caster sugar
6fl oz (175ml) water, warmed
¼ oz (7g) low-fat, freeze-dried milk
  powder
9oz (250g) strong plain white flour,
  sifted
¼ oz (7g) saffron, ground and soaked
  for several hours in 2 teaspoons
  warm water
a large pinch of salt
2½ oz (65g) butter, softened
2½–3oz (65–75g) currants
1½–2oz (40–50g) mixed candied
  peel

Cream together the yeast and caster sugar and mix with the warm water, milk powder and 1oz (25g) of the flour. Whisk, then leave in a warm place for 30 minutes until frothy and doubled in size. Strain the saffron, add with all the other ingredients to the yeast mixture and beat well to a fairly elastic dough. Leave in a warm place for a further 40–50 minutes until doubled in size. Grease a 2lb (900g) loaf tin. Turn the mixture into the tin and stand in a warm place for 30 minutes to rise almost to the top of the tin. Meanwhile heat the oven to gas mark 4/350°F/180°C. When the dough has risen, bake for 50 minutes to 1 hour until a skewer comes out clean. Remove from the oven and turn out on to a wire rack to cool.

This saffron loaf is not very sweet and, spread with butter and honey or preserves, it makes an ideal tea bread.

Simnel Cake

Makes 1 × 8in (20cm)
round cake

1lb 4oz (550g) marzipan
6oz (175g) butter, softened
5oz (150g) light soft brown sugar
3 eggs, beaten
½ oz (15g) glycerine
½ oz (15g) glucose
4oz (100g) strong plain white flour
2oz (50g) ordinary plain white flour
1oz (25g) ground almonds
1 teaspoon mixed spice
½ teaspoon grated nutmeg
12oz (350g) sultanas
9oz (250g) currants
4oz (100g) mixed candied peel
a little apricot jam for fixing the
  marzipan topping in place

Preheat the oven to gas mark 4/350°F/180°C. Grease an 8in (20cm) round tin, line with a double layer of greaseproof paper and grease well. Divide the marzipan into three portions, one slightly smaller than the other two. Set the smallest portion aside and, on a sugared board, roll out one of the two equal portions to a circle just smaller than the diameter of the tin. Beat together the butter and sugar until light and fluffy. Add the beaten eggs, glycerine and glucose and beat again. Mix together the flour, almonds and spices and gradually add to the mixture, stirring gently to blend. Do not beat. Add the dried fruit and fold gently in. Turn half the mixture into the prepared tin and smooth the top. Place the circle of marzipan on top and then cover with the remaining cake mixture. Smooth the top and bake for 1 hour (if the top starts to become too brown, cover with a double layer of greaseproof paper), then reduce the oven temperature to gas mark 3/325°F/160°C and bake for a further 45 minutes to 1 hour until a skewer comes out clean. Remove from the oven and leave to cool in the tin for about 15 minutes before turning out on to a wire rack to cool completely. When cold, brush the top with apricot jam. Roll out the second portion of marzipan to make a circle to fit the top of the cake. Put it in place and press gently to make sure it is firmly fixed. Form the remaining marzipan into eleven small balls and arrange them around the rim of the cake, sticking them on with a little apricot jam. Turn the grill to a moderate heat and place the cake underneath for a few minutes until the marzipan just begins to brown. To serve, wrap a wide yellow satin ribbon around the cake and fix with a pin. Arrange a small posy of fresh spring flowers on the top.

Simnel cakes were originally made for Mothering Sunday, the fourth Sunday in Lent, but today they are more often eaten on Easter Sunday. It was the custom for children who were working away from home to return to their families on Mothering Sunday in order to worship with them in the mother church. They would bring a cake for their mother, often made by their employer's wife. The name probably derives from the Latin word simila, meaning fine flour, and there is a possibility that the cake dates back to the Roman occupation of Britain. Another theory is that it stems from the Anglo-Saxon word symel, meaning a feast. Mothering Sunday was a recognised relaxation from the Lenten fast and was also sometimes called Refreshment Sunday. The eleven balls of marzipan around the edge of the cake represent eleven of the apostles; Judas is missing.

A Chinese mystic of the T'ang Dynasty wrote:
'The first cup of tea moistens my lips and throat. The second shatters my loneliness. The third causes the wrongs of life to fade gently from my recollection. The fourth purifies my soul. The fifth lifts me to the realms of the unwinking gods.'

KILLERTON

Sir Thomas Dyke Acland's decision to engage the Scottish gardener John Veitch to lay out the grounds round his new house at Killerton in the 1770s was an inspired one. Then a young man, Veitch was to become one of the greatest nurserymen and landscape designers of his day. His garden at Killerton is laid out on the slopes of the steep volcanic outcrop known as Killerton Clump. (In Saxon times it was called Dolbury, and it still gives its name to the popular pudding and cake which are served in the restaurant.)

Although the house does not compete with its surroundings, Killerton's interiors, much altered over the years, recall country living between the First and Second World Wars, when weekend parties sat down to eat off the family silver laid out in the dining-room, the most privileged female guests nearest the fire. While the Acland family was in residence, tea was always served in the music-room, and there is some exquisite porcelain on display in the cabinets, including some Chinese tea bowls and teapots, eighteenth-century Derby and Worcester, and some fine French and German pieces.

Many of the rooms are now devoted to the Paulise de Bush collection of eighteenth- to twentieth-century costume, among which are some fine tea gowns, popular in the late nineteenth century as a comfortable afternoon garment to wear at home. A typical tea gown was made of white cotton or linen trimmed with broderie anglaise, tucks and frills.

Dolbury Cake

Makes 1 × 7in (17·5cm) square cake

4oz (100g) margarine, softened
1½oz (40g) white Flora, softened
5oz (150g) light or dark soft brown sugar
3 eggs
8oz (225g) cooking or eating apples, peeled, cored and chopped
8oz (225g) mincemeat
8oz (225g) self-raising flour, sifted
2–3fl oz (50–75ml) milk

Preheat the oven to gas mark 3/325°F/160°C. Grease and line a 7in (17·5cm) square tin. Beat together the fats and sugar. Beat in the eggs, one at a time, whisking well after each. Add the apple, mincemeat and flour and mix carefully. Add enough of the milk to give a soft, moist consistency. Turn into the prepared tin and bake for 1½ hours until a skewer comes out clean. Remove from the oven and leave to cool in the tin for 15 minutes before turning out on to a wire rack to cool completely.

This is a soft, moist cake with a slightly spicy flavour.

Wholemeal Fruit Scones

Makes approximately 20–22 scones

1lb (450g) strong plain wholemeal
  flour, sifted
1 tablespoon baking powder
3½oz (90g) margarine
2oz (50g) white Flora
a pinch of salt
½ teaspoon ground cinnamon

½ teaspoon grated nutmeg
2oz (50g) mixed dried fruit
  (currants, raisins, peel)
3oz (75g) sultanas
2oz (50g) light soft brown sugar
2 eggs
4–5fl oz (100–150ml) milk

Preheat the oven to gas mark 7/425°F/220°C. Grease two baking trays. Mix together the flour and baking powder and rub in the fats so that the mixture resembles fine breadcrumbs. Add the salt, spices, dried fruit and sugar and stir well. Beat the eggs. Add to the dry ingredients and mix with enough of the milk to give a soft dough. On a lightly floured board, pat out to a thickness of ¾in (1·5cm) and cut into rounds using a 2½in (6cm) cutter. Place on the prepared trays and bake for 15 minutes until golden brown and firm. Remove from the oven and lift on to a wire rack to cool.

KINGSTON LACY

Home of the Bankes family from 1663, when Sir Ralph Bankes built a house here to replace the earlier seat at Corfe Castle, Kingston Lacy is a monument to the eccentric and original William John Bankes (1786-1855), friend of Byron. With the aid of Sir Charles Barry, architect of the Houses of Parliament, William transformed the house into an Italianate palazzo, filled with pictures and works of art he acquired during his extensive travels in the Mediterranean. A broad Italianate terrace on the south front sweeps right across the façade, and the wide marble staircase leading up to the principal rooms on the first floor is also of Italian inspiration, provided with an airy loggia on the half-landing. One of three bronze figures set in niches here depicts Lady Mary Bankes, still holding the key of Corfe Castle which she twice defended for King Charles in the Civil War (the actual keys hang in the library upstairs).

The drawing-room is filled with the Edwardian objects placed there by Henrietta Bankes, mother of the late Ralph Bankes who bequeathed Kingston Lacy to the National Trust. The room is laid out as it was in 1900, including a silver tea service on a tray with a kettle on its burner. Until the late nineteenth century tea was a relatively expensive commodity; in order to prevent the servants pilfering surplus supplies, decorative caddies containing tea for everyday use were kept in the drawing-room or salon, under the careful protection of the lady of the house. At tea-time it was her responsibility to brew the tea; a tea kettle, with its own stand and burner, was therefore essential.

Florentine Slice

Makes 16 slices

*12oz (350g) good quality milk or
  plain chocolate*
*12oz (350g) mixed dried fruit
  (raisins, sultanas, currants, peel)*
4oz (100g) glacé cherries

4oz (100g) shredded coconut
4oz (100g) caster sugar
2oz (50g) butter, melted
2 eggs, beaten

Line an 11 × 8in (27·5 × 20cm) tin with foil. Melt the chocolate and spread evenly in the base of the tin. Leave to cool in the refrigerator until set. Preheat the oven to gas mark 4/350°F/180°C. Mix together the dried fruit, glacé cherries, coconut, sugar, butter and beaten eggs and spread evenly over the chocolate. Bake for 25 minutes until golden brown. Remove from the oven and leave to cool in the tin. When cool, place the tin in the refrigerator until really cold. Cut into fingers and turn out of the tin.

This rich, gooey cake contains no flour, so is ideal for people who cannot eat wheat.

Honey Tea Bread

Makes 1 × 2lb (900g) loaf

FOR THE LOAF
8oz (225g) mixed dried fruit
5fl oz (150ml) cold tea
4oz (100g) clear honey

8oz (225g) self-raising flour, sifted
1 egg, well beaten
4oz (100g) butter, melted

FOR THE TOPPING
1 tablespoon honey, warmed
*1oz (25g) finely chopped nuts
  (walnuts, hazelnuts or almonds)*

1oz (25g) demerara sugar

Place the dried fruit, tea and honey in a bowl and leave to soak overnight or for at least 6 hours. Preheat the oven to gas mark 2/300°F/150°C. Grease and line a 2lb (900g) loaf tin. Mix the flour into the fruit mixture. Add the beaten egg and beat hard. Finally, beat in the melted butter. Turn into the prepared tin and bake for 50 minutes. Remove from the oven and prepare the topping. Brush with the warmed honey, mix together the nuts and sugar and sprinkle over the top. Return to the oven and bake for a further 15–20 minutes until a skewer comes out clean. Remove from the oven and leave to cool in the tin. When cool, carefully remove from the tin and serve sliced with butter.

LANHYDROCK

Lanhydrock is a beautiful house with many special features: fine and extensive grounds, a Jacobean gatehouse, forty-nine rooms open to the public and magnificent kitchens. When the original seventeenth-century house was partly destroyed in 1881 by a fire that started in the main kitchen chimney, the Robartes family who owned Lanhydrock took the opportunity to plan and rebuild kitchens which were of a suitable size and which had every possible up-to-date appliance and convenience, including fire-proofing. The high ceiling with its tall windows allowed heat and odours to escape; a closed range with a variety of spits was suited to different methods of cooking enough food for the large household; and a carefully planned series of smaller rooms leading off the main kitchen ensured the efficient running of the domestic quarters. There is a scullery where vegetables were prepared and kitchen pots were washed; a dairy with marble slabs for cooling the milk, cream, butter, moulded puddings and cheeses; a bakehouse with an oven which took four days to heat and which still works today; and a fish larder, a meat larder and a dry larder.

Throughout the house little touches give a lived-in feeling. No sound comes from the servants' quarters, where a pair of black lace-up boots stands neatly by a bed and a piece of knitting has been put down beside a chair. Two floors below, pipes lie waiting in the masculine confines of the smoking-room, and the dining-room table is laid for ten, the menu handwritten in French. The morning-room is set each morning with a tray of sherry and sherry glasses, as it would have been when the family was living there. In the boudoir, the table is set with French china, silver tea knives, linen napkins, a beehive honey pot, a silver jam pot, silver teaspoons and butterpats in a silver dish, all laid out on a lace cloth ready for afternoon tea. The period feeling is so strong that it would be no surprise to meet a scurrying maid with a tray or to hear the Robartes family and their guests returning from a stroll.

Stands the Church clock at ten to three?
And is there honey still for tea?

Rupert Brooke (1887-1915), 'The Old Vicarage, Grantchester'

Apricot Sesame Slice

Makes 12 slices

FOR THE BASE
4oz (100g) margarine
4oz (100g) golden syrup
4oz (100g) demerara sugar
8oz (225g) porridge oats
4oz (100g) shredded coconut
2oz (50g) sesame seeds, untoasted

3 teaspoons ground cinnamon
a pinch of salt
4oz (100g) dried apricots, roughly
  chopped
4oz (100g) chocolate chips
  (milk or plain)

FOR THE TOPPING
1oz (25g) sesame seeds, untoasted

Preheat the oven to gas mark 2/300°F/150°C. Grease an 8 × 11in (20 × 27·5cm) tin. Melt the margarine and syrup together in a large pan. Add the sugar, oats, coconut, sesame seeds, cinnamon, salt and apricots and stir well, making sure that all the ingredients are evenly distributed. Stir in the chocolate chips and mix thoroughly. Turn into the prepared tin and press well down. Smooth the top and sprinkle with the 1oz (25g) sesame seeds. Press well into the mixture and bake for 30-35 minutes until golden and firm. Remove from the oven and leave to cool in the tin. When cold, cut into squares or slices.

Chocolate Digestives

Makes 22-24 biscuits

4oz (100g) fine oatmeal
4oz (100g) plain wholemeal flour,
  sifted
2½oz (65g) caster or granulated
  sugar
a small pinch of bicarbonate of soda

a small pinch of salt
4½oz (115g) butter or margarine,
  softened
1 egg, beaten
6oz (175g) plain or milk chocolate
  for spreading

Preheat the oven to gas mark 3/325°F/160°C. Grease two baking trays. Mix together the oatmeal, flour, sugar, bicarbonate of soda and salt and rub in the fat (this is best done in a food processor, if you have one). Add the beaten egg and bind together to a stiff dough. Sprinkle plenty of oatmeal on to a board and roll out the dough to a thickness of approximately ¼in (0·5cm). Using a 2½in (6cm) cutter, cut into rounds. Place on the prepared trays and bake for 15-20 minutes until pale golden. Remove from the oven and lift carefully on to a wire rack to cool. Melt the chocolate and dip the tops of the biscuits in. (It may be easier to spread the chocolate on to the biscuits with a palette knife.) Place on a wire rack with the chocolate side uppermost and leave to set in the refrigerator or in a cool place. Alternatively, leave plain and eat with cheese.

Cornish Banana Cake

Makes 1 × double layer
7in (17·5cm) round cake

FOR THE CAKE

8oz (225g) very ripe bananas
   (weighed after peeling)
3½oz (90g) caster sugar
3½oz (90g) butter, softened
7oz (200g) self-raising flour, sifted
1 egg

½ teaspoon bicarbonate of soda
1 tablespoon milk
whole, blanched almonds, half
   walnuts or slices of dried banana
chips to decorate

FOR THE FILLING

1 ripe banana
2oz (50g) butter, softened

2oz (50g) caster sugar

FOR THE ICING

1oz (25g) cocoa powder, sifted
8oz (225g) icing sugar, sifted

1 soft, very ripe banana

Preheat the oven to gas mark 4/350°F/140°C. Grease two 7in (17·5cm) round sandwich tins. Mash the bananas and sugar together in a food processor or mixer. Beat in the butter, and add the flour and egg alternately. Dissolve the bicarbonate of soda in the milk and add to the mixture. Beat well to a fairly sticky batter. Turn into the prepared tins, smooth the tops and bake for 35–40 minutes until the sponge springs back when lightly pressed. Remove from the oven and turn on to a wire rack to cool. To make the filling, beat all the ingredients together until well mixed and use to sandwich the cakes together. For the icing, beat the ingredients together until dark and really smooth and spread on to the top of the cake. Decorate with the blanched almonds, walnut halves or dried banana chips.

Cornish Splits

Makes 12 splits

2oz (50g) fresh yeast
1½oz (40g) caster sugar
just under 1 pint (600ml) warm
   milk and water mixed

2lb (900g) strong plain white flour,
   sifted
1 egg, beaten

Grease two baking trays. Mix together the yeast, sugar and warm milk and water. Leave in a warm place for about 20–30 minutes until frothy. Add the liquid to the flour with the beaten egg and mix to a soft dough. Knead until smooth and elastic. Leave in a warm place for about an hour until doubled in size. Knock back, knead again and divide into 3oz (75g) pieces. Mould with the hands into neat bun shapes, place on the prepared trays and leave in a warm place for about 20 minutes until well risen. Meanwhile heat the oven to gas mark 3/325°F/160°C. When the splits are well risen, bake for 20–25 minutes until they just start to turn brown. Remove from the oven and cool on a wire rack. To serve, split and fill with jam and clotted cream and dust the tops with icing sugar.

MONTACUTE HOUSE

Montacute is every inch an Elizabethan house, the product of a confident and enquiring age. It was designed for the successful lawyer Sir Edward Phelips, later Master of the Rolls and Chancellor to the Household of Henry, Prince of Wales. Probably finished by 1601, it is an H-shaped building of local honey-brown ham stone.

Although hardly any of the original contents survived the decline in the Phelipses' fortunes, leading to Montacute's sale in 1929, fine furniture and tapestries from the Sir Malcolm Stewart bequest give the rooms an authentic atmosphere. In the medieval-style great hall two rare early seventeenth-century plaster panels illustrate village life, one showing a hen-pecked husband being berated by his wife as he draws beer from a barrel rather than attending to the baby he clasps in his left arm.

An inventory from 1728 shows that what is now the library once contained two tea tables, and no doubt from that date onwards the Phelips family would have taken tea regularly in the morning for breakfast and late at night as a nightcap, as well as drinking it in the afternoon with callers.

Ginger Flapjack

Makes 10–12 pieces

FOR THE FLAPJACK
6oz (175g) butter
1oz (25g) golden syrup
4oz (100g) light soft brown sugar

8oz (225g) porridge oats
2oz (50g) shredded coconut
1 teaspoon ground ginger

FOR THE TOPPING
6–8oz (175–225g) icing sugar, sifted

1 teaspoon ground ginger
1–2 tablespoons cold water

Preheat the oven to gas mark 4/350°F/180°C. Grease a 7 × 11in (17·5 × 27·5cm) Swiss roll tin. Melt together the butter, syrup and sugar. Stir in the oats, coconut and ginger and mix well. Turn into the prepared tin and bake for 20 minutes until golden and firm. Remove from the oven and leave to cool in the tin. When cold, prepare the topping by mixing together the icing sugar, ginger and water. Spread the icing over the flapjack and leave to set. Cut into pieces and lift carefully from the tin.

Pineapple Upside-Down Cake

Makes 1 × 6in (15cm) round cake

6oz (175g) golden syrup
8oz (225g) tinned pineapple slices, drained
4oz (100g) butter, softened
4oz (100g) caster sugar

2 eggs, beaten
4oz (100g) self-raising flour, sifted
a pinch of salt
a pinch of ground cinnamon

Preheat the oven to gas mark 3/325°F/160°C. Grease and line a 6in (15cm) round tin. Spread the syrup in the base of the tin and arrange the pineapple slices over the top. Beat together the butter and sugar until light and fluffy. Beat in the eggs, one at a time, adding 1 tablespoon of flour with each. Beat hard, then fold in the remaining flour with the salt and cinnamon. Mix well without beating. Turn into the prepared tin and bake for 1¼ hours until a skewer comes out clean. Remove from the oven and leave to cool in the tin. When cold, turn out and serve with the pineapple side uppermost.

ST MICHAEL'S MOUNT

St Michael's Mount rises from the sea off the Cornish coast, its dramatic profile crowned by Arthurian battlements and towers. This strange hybrid is part religious retreat, part fortress, part elegant country house. Associated with Christianity since the fifth century, it became an important place of pilgrimage in the Middle Ages. The heart of the castle today is a fourteenth-century granite church, the major survival from the Benedictine priory established here in the twelfth century.

The guardroom in the entry range, the garrison room embedded in the rock, an old sentry box overlooking the steep cobbled path up to the castle and gun batteries pointing out to sea recall the 200 years when St Michael's Mount was a manned fortress, a major link in England's defences against the Spanish Armada and a Royalist stronghold in the Civil War until the castle's surrender in 1646. The last military governor, the Parliamentarian Colonel John St Aubyn, began the conversion of the fortress into a private house; 300 years later his descendants still live here. Sir John St Aubyn, 3rd Baronet, transformed the ruined lady chapel into the elegant blue drawing-room; it is here that you can imagine trays of tea being served while the sun streams in through the Gothic windows.

Chocolate Rum Cake

Makes 1 × 8in (20cm) round cake

FOR THE CAKE

9oz (250g) margarine, softened
9oz (250g) caster sugar
4 eggs
9oz (250g) self-raising flour, sifted
4oz (100g) drinking chocolate
   powder

1½ oz (40g) cocoa powder, sifted
a few drops of vanilla essence
2-3 tablespoons dark rum
5fl oz (150ml) milk

FOR THE FILLING AND ICING

18oz (500g) icing sugar, sifted
1½ oz (40g) cocoa powder, sifted
8oz (225g) butter or margarine,
   softened

6oz (175g) caster sugar
2 tablespoons dark rum
2½ fl oz (65ml) milk

Preheat the oven to gas mark 2/300°F/150°C. Grease and line an 8in (20cm) round tin. Beat together the margarine and sugar until light and fluffy. Beat in the eggs, one at a time, beating hard after each addition. Combine the flour, drinking chocolate and cocoa and add to the mixture. Mix in carefully, taking care not to beat in any more air or the cake will flood over the top of the tin during cooking. Add the vanilla essence, rum and enough milk to mix to a soft, dropping consistency. Turn into the prepared tin, smooth the top and hollow out the middle a little. Bake for 1½-1¾ hours until a skewer comes out clean. Remove from the oven and allow to cool in the tin for about 15 minutes before turning on to a wire rack to cool completely. To make the icing and filling, beat all the ingredients together until light and fluffy. Cut the cake horizontally through the middle. Spread half the mixture on to the base and sandwich the other half of the cake on top. Spread the remaining filling on top of the cake and decorate with grated chocolate, half walnuts or by making a pattern with the prongs of a fork.

This is an impressive, deep cake which looks and tastes delicious.

Cornish Fairings

Makes approximately 26 biscuits

4oz (100g) margarine
4oz (100g) granulated sugar
4oz (100g) golden syrup
8oz (225g) plain flour, sifted
1 teaspoon baking powder

1 teaspoon bicarbonate of soda
1 teaspoon ground ginger
1 teaspoon mixed spice
1 teaspoon ground cinnamon

Preheat the oven to gas mark 2/300°F/150°C. Grease two or three baking trays. Put the margarine, sugar and syrup into a small pan and melt gently together until the sugar is dissolved. Mix together the dry ingredients and add the sugar mixture. Mix to a soft dough. Form the dough into balls weighing approximately ¾oz (22g) and place on the prepared trays, leaving plenty of room for the biscuits to spread while cooking. Press each ball down lightly and bake for 10–15 minutes until golden. Remove from the oven and leave to cool on the trays for 5 minutes before lifting carefully on to a wire rack to cool completely.

At fairgrounds in the past, travelling salesmen often sold little bags of delicacies containing such things as spiced biscuits, caraway comfits, candied angelica, macaroons and almond sweetmeats. Gradually, over the years, the cakes and biscuits were sold as separate items and became known as fairings.

Easter Biscuits

Makes 10 biscuits

FOR THE BISCUITS
6oz (175g) plain flour, sifted
2oz (50g) rice flour
1 teaspoon mixed spice
4oz (100g) butter, softened
4oz (100g) caster sugar

2 egg yolks
3oz (75g) currants
1 tablespoon brandy
½ tablespoon milk

FOR THE TOPPING
2 egg whites, lightly beaten

2 tablespoons caster sugar

Preheat the oven to gas mark 4/350°F/180°C. Grease two baking trays. Mix together the flour, rice flour and mixed spice. Beat together the butter and sugar until light and fluffy. Beat in the egg yolks, one at a time. Add the currants, flour mixture, brandy and milk and mix to a stiff dough. Turn on to a lightly floured board and knead gently until smooth. Roll out to a thickness of ¼in (0·5cm) and cut into rounds using a 4in (10cm) fluted cutter. Place on the prepared trays and brush with plenty of beaten egg white. Sprinkle with caster sugar and bake for 15–20 minutes until crisp and pale golden. Remove from the oven and leave to cool on the trays for 5 minutes before lifting carefully on to a wire rack to cool completely.

These are light biscuits with a subtle spice and brandy flavour and a delicious crunchy topping.

There is a great deal of poetry and fine sentiment in a chest of tea.

Ralph Waldo Emerson (1803-83), *Letters and Social Aims*

THE SPREAD EAGLE INN

The fine house of Stourhead on a ridge of the Wiltshire Downs is over-shadowed by the magical garden created in a steep-sided combe which falls away to the west. Sheltered and enclosed by windbreaks planted along the rim of the valley, the perfect eighteenth-century landscape preserved here looks inward, with views over wooded slopes to the serene artificial lake in the depths of the combe. A number of little classical temples along the shore are framed against the trees in a sequence of contrived vistas which shift and change according to the viewpoint on the path around the lake. Primarily the creation of Henry Hoare II, son of the London banker who built the Palladian house, Stourhead is designed as a series of experiences and is never the same however often it is visited.

Although Henry Hoare originally hid the estate village on the edge of the valley behind a screen of trees so that it would not intrude on his design, the row of tiled cottages stretching down to the classical bridge over an arm of the lake adds to the overall charm. Opposite is the medieval parish church, and nearby is the Spread Eagle Inn. Henry Hoare built the inn in the eighteenth century to accommodate some of the visitors who came to admire his famous garden, and it retains many historic features, including Georgian and Regency fireplaces, and a vaulted beer and wine cellar in the basement. The Spread Eagle still provides accommodation, run as a hotel and restaurant on behalf of the National Trust.

Blackmore Vale Cake

Makes 1 × 2lb (900g) loaf

4oz (100g) butter, softened
4oz (100g) light or dark soft brown sugar
5fl oz (150ml) milk
1 dessertspoon black treacle

1 teaspoon bicarbonate of soda
12oz (350g) plain flour, sifted
3oz (75g) mixed candied peel
12oz (350g) raisins

Preheat the oven to gas mark 2/300°F/150°C. Grease and line a 2lb (900g) loaf tin. Beat together the butter and sugar until light and fluffy. Warm the milk and add the treacle and bicarbonate of soda. Mix thoroughly and add with the flour to the beaten butter and sugar. Beat well. Fold in the peel and raisins and mix well. Turn into the prepared tin and bake for 2¼–2½ hours until a skewer comes out clean. Remove from the oven and turn out on to a wire rack to cool.

This cake has been served at meets of the Blackmore Vale Hunt for over a hundred years.

Plum Loaf

Makes 1 × 2lb (900g) loaf

8oz (225g) fresh plums, stoned (weighed after stoning)
4oz (100g) butter, softened
2oz (50g) light soft brown sugar
2 tablespoons golden syrup
2 eggs
8oz (225g) self-raising flour, sifted
2 teaspoons mixed spice
a little milk
caster sugar for dusting

Preheat the oven to gas mark 4/350°F/180°C. Grease and line a 2lb (900g) loaf tin. Chop the plums coarsely. Beat together the butter, sugar and syrup until light and fluffy. Add the eggs one at a time with a little flour, beating hard after each addition. Fold in the remaining flour, the spice and plums and enough milk to mix to a soft, dropping consistency. Turn into the prepared tin and bake for 1¼ hours until a skewer comes out clean. Remove from the oven and turn out on to a wire rack to cool. Before serving, dust with caster sugar.

This is an unusual cake and an excellent way to use spare fresh plums. The fruit gives the loaf a soft, moist texture and the spicy flavour complements the taste of the plums. Eat freshly baked, as the cake tends to dry out if left.

TRELISSICK

Trelissick is set in Daphne du Maurier country. The estate stands at the head of the great estuary of the River Fal, a ribbon of deep water running far inland with smaller creeks and inlets branching off on either side. Woods of oak with areas of beech and pine clothe the slopes leading down to the water, hanging over the tidal mudflats in the creeks. It is easy to imagine smugglers here, with little boats coming into these lonely inlets under cover of darkness. Below the house the romantically named King Harry Ferry is the only connection across the water to the Roseland Peninsula on the other side.

The present garden has been largely created by Mr and Mrs Ronald Copeland since 1937. They planted many of the species that flourish in the mild Cornish air, including the rhododendrons and azaleas which are now such a feature of the garden, hydrangeas, camellias and flowering cherries, and exotics such as the ginkgo and various species of palm. They also ensured that the blossoms they nurtured had a wider, if unknowing, audience. Mr Copeland was chairman and later managing director of his family's business, the Spode china factory, and flowers grown at Trelissick were used as models for those painted on ware produced at the works.

Blackberry Tea Bread

Makes 1 × 2lb (900g) loaf

12oz (350g) plain flour, sifted
1 teaspoon mixed spice
6oz (175g) margarine, softened
6oz (175g) caster sugar
8oz (225g) fresh or frozen
    blackberries (if frozen, use
    straight from the freezer)

the rind and juice of 1 lemon
1 tablespoon black treacle
2 eggs, beaten
½ teaspoon bicarbonate of soda
2 tablespoons milk

Preheat the oven to gas mark 4/350°F/180°C. Grease and line a 2lb (900g) loaf tin. Mix together the flour and mixed spice and rub in the margarine until the mixture bears a resemblance to fine breadcrumbs. Add the sugar, blackberries, lemon juice and rind, treacle and eggs and mix well. Dissolve the bicarbonate of soda in the milk, add to the mixture and beat well. Pour into the prepared tin, level and bake for 45 minutes. Reduce the oven temperature to gas mark 2/300°F/150°C and cook for a further 30–45 minutes until a skewer comes out clean. Remove from the oven and leave in the tin for about 15 minutes before turning out on to a wire rack to cool.

This unusual loaf is an ideal and novel way of using the blackberries that flourish in our hedgerows every summer.

Macaroons

Makes 18–20 macaroons

2 egg whites
4oz (100g) ground almonds
7oz (200g) caster sugar
1oz (25g) granulated sugar

½ oz (15g) rice flour
1 teaspoon almond essence
whole or split blanched almonds
    to decorate

Preheat the oven to gas mark 4/350°F/180°C. Cover three baking trays with sheets of rice paper or non-stick greaseproof paper. Beat the egg whites for 3–4 minutes with an electric beater. Leave to rest for 4–5 minutes, then beat again until thick and white. Fold in the remaining ingredients and place the mixture in a piping bag fitted with a plain ½in (1cm) nozzle. Pipe small circles of the mixture on to the paper, leaving room for the macaroons to spread. Place a whole or split almond in the middle of each and bake for 10–15 minutes until pale golden. Remove from the oven and leave to cool on the trays. If using rice paper, cut round each macaroon. If using non-stick greaseproof paper, the macaroons should lift off easily.

Peanut and Orange Cookies

Makes approximately
18 cookies

4oz (100g) margarine
3oz (75g) light soft brown sugar
1oz (25g) golden syrup
1 tablespoon crunchy peanut butter

4oz (100g) self-raising flour, sifted
2oz (50g) rolled oats
the grated rind of 1 orange
1oz (25g) salted peanuts, chopped

Preheat the oven to gas mark 3/325°F/160°C. Grease two baking trays. Put the margarine, sugar, syrup and peanut butter into a small pan and heat gently until melted. Mix together the flour, oats and orange rind and make a well in the centre. Pour in the melted ingredients and mix thoroughly. Form dessertspoonfuls of the mixture into balls and place on the prepared trays, leaving sufficient room for the biscuits to spread. Press flat with the palm of the hand and sprinkle the tops with chopped peanuts. Bake for 15–20 minutes until pale golden. Remove from the oven and leave to cool on the trays for a few minutes before lifting carefully on to a wire rack to cool completely.

TRERICE

This delightful Elizabethan house built of local buff-coloured limestone retained its original charm and escaped modernisation during the prosperous eighteenth and nineteenth centuries, the heyday of the Cornish mining industries, perhaps because its owners chose to live elsewhere. It passed in 1802 from the Arundells, one of the great families of Cornwall, to the Aclands, whose principal estates were in Devon and Somerset.

The glory of Trerice is the sunny, south-facing drawing-room on the first floor, which Sir John Arundell probably created out of a medieval solar. The room is richly decorated with bold Elizabethan plasterwork over the fireplace and on the splendid barrel ceiling, one of the best of the period in the West Country. Although none of the furniture in the house is original, there are some good oak and walnut pieces, including a long-case clock by Thomas Tompion. Cabinets in the musicians' gallery display some beautiful blue and white Worcester and Caughly porcelain and part of a Salopian china tea service.

There are also some fine examples of Chinese export tea ware. Porcelain tea bowls and pots began arriving in Britain with the early cargoes of tea. Sailors and ships' officers bartered iron and silver bars in the Chinese ports for porcelain to bring home. They were allowed to bring anything they liked as long as it was stowed in the hold of the ship, and they also had the right to trade privately. European potters were amazed by the fine, translucent quality of the Chinese ware and spent the following fifty years attempting to manufacture something similar.

Abbeys

Makes 16 biscuits

FOR THE BISCUITS
4oz (100g) margarine, softened
4oz (100g) caster sugar
1 teaspoon golden syrup
4oz (100g) self-raising flour, sifted

4oz (100g) porridge oats
½ tablespoon full-cream milk
  powder (Coffeemate or similar)
½ teaspoon bicarbonate of soda

FOR THE COATING
10oz (275g) plain or milk chocolate

Preheat the oven to gas mark 2/300°F/150°C. Grease two baking trays. Beat together the margarine, sugar and syrup until light and fluffy. Add the other ingredients and work together. Form the mixture into balls weighing approximately 1oz (25g) and place on the prepared trays. Press down slightly with the palm of the hand and bake for 20 minutes until pale golden. Remove from the oven and leave to cool on the trays for a few minutes before lifting on to a wire rack to cool completely. Melt the chocolate in a narrow but deep container (a cup or small bowl) and dip the biscuits into the chocolate so that half of each biscuit is coated. Place carefully on the wire rack or on greaseproof paper and leave to set.

These are excellent served with ice-cream or other light desserts, as well as being perfect with morning coffee or afternoon tea.

Fatless Tea Bread

Makes 1 × 2lb (900g) loaf

1lb (450g) mixed dried fruit
  (raisins, sultanas, currants, peel
  and dates)
10fl oz (300ml) cold tea

10oz (275g) self-raising wholemeal
  flour, sifted
5oz (150g) light or dark soft
  brown sugar
1 egg

Preheat the oven to gas mark 3/325°F/160°C. Grease and line a 2lb (900g) loaf tin. Mix all the ingredients together so that they are evenly distributed. Turn into the prepared tin and bake for 2 hours until a skewer comes out clean. Remove from the oven and turn out on to a wire rack to cool. Serve sliced and spread with butter.

This is an excellent cake for anybody who is conscious of their cholesterol intake. There is no fat at all and most of the sweetness comes from the dried fruit.

Hot Cross Buns

Makes 18 buns

FOR THE BUNS
1oz (25g) fresh yeast
2oz (50g) caster sugar
15fl oz (400ml) milk and water,
    mixed and warmed
2oz (50g) margarine, softened
1½lb (675g) strong plain white
    flour, sifted

a pinch of salt
8oz (225g) mixed dried fruit
4oz (100g) mixed candied peel
2 teaspoons mixed spice
2 teaspoons grated nutmeg

FOR THE TOPPING
1 tablespoon caster sugar
1 tablespoon cold water

thick paste made with 3oz (75g)
    plain flour and 3 tablespoons
    water (or trimmings from
    short pastry)

Cream the yeast with the sugar and add 5fl oz (150ml) of the milk and water mixture. Stir well then leave in a warm place for 20-30 minutes until frothy. Grease three baking trays. Rub the margarine into the flour and add the salt, mixed dried fruit, peel, mixed spice and nutmeg. When the yeast mixture is frothy, add to the dry ingredients with the remaining milk and water. Mix to a stiff dough and knead on a floured board until smooth. Form the dough into 3oz (75g) balls and place on the prepared trays. Leave in a warm place for about 30 minutes until almost doubled in size. Meanwhile preheat the oven to gas mark 7/425°F/220°C. Mix together the caster sugar and water for the topping. Make the stiff paste with the flour and water and roll out on a floured board. Cut narrow strips ready to make the crosses for the tops of the buns. When the buns have risen, carefully brush the tops with sugar and water and place a cross on each. Bake for 15 minutes until nicely browned. Remove from the oven and lift on to a wire rack to cool. Serve warm with butter.

The tradition of baking special cakes for Good Friday has its origins in pre-Christian times when many cultures offered cakes marked with a cross to their various gods and goddesses. As with so many rituals and symbols of pre-Christian religions, the cross was adopted into Christianity to represent Christ's cross. In the days when bread and buns were baked at home, one hot cross bun was kept and hung above the stove to ward off evil spirits until the next batch was baked twelve months later. The bun was believed to have powerful medicinal qualities, so crumbs from it were mixed into home remedies for family and livestock throughout the year.

Sesame Rolls

Makes approximately
14 rolls

½ oz (15g) fresh yeast
2 teaspoons caster sugar
15 fl oz (400ml) water, warmed
1½ lb (675g) strong plain white
    flour, sifted
1½ teaspoons Coffeemate or similar
    full-cream milk powder

½ teaspoon salt
1oz (25g) margarine, softened
1 egg, beaten, mixed with a little
    water
2–3 tablespoons sesame seeds

Mix together the yeast, sugar and 3fl oz (75ml) of the water. Leave in a warm place for about 20–30 minutes until frothy. Mix together the flour, milk powder and salt and rub in the fat. Add the yeast mixture and the remaining water and mix to a pliable dough. Knead until smooth and elastic, then place in a bowl, cover with a damp cloth and leave in a warm place for 1–1½ hours until doubled in size. Grease two baking trays. When the dough is well risen, divide into 2½oz (65g) pieces, form these into bun shapes and place on the prepared trays. Brush the tops with eggwash and sprinkle liberally with sesame seeds. Leave in a warm place for about 30 minutes until well risen. Meanwhile heat the oven to gas mark 6/400°F/200°C. When the rolls are well risen, bake for 20–25 minutes until golden brown and firm. Remove from the oven and lift on to a wire rack to cool. Serve warm or cold.

If liked stir a tablespoon of sesame seeds into the dough with the yeast mixture. Sprinkle as above with more seeds before baking.

A Drawing Room Tea, clockwise from the top: cheese and celery whirls (page 92); date and cinnamon shortbread (page 49); Walsingham honey cake (page 75).

THE VYNE

The building of this long, low, U-shaped red-brick house was started by Lord Sandys before he began his long career in the service of Henry VIII culminating in his appointment to the office of Lord Chamberlain in 1526. Lord Sandys's loyalty was rewarded at the Dissolution of the Monasteries with the gift of Mottisfont Abbey, also in Hampshire, and it was here that the family retired when impoverishment in the Civil War forced the sale of The Vyne in 1653.

The new owner was another successful and astute politician, Chaloner Chute, who reduced the size of the house and added the classical portico on the north front, thought to be the earliest on a domestic building. Chute's great-grandson, John, friend of Horace Walpole, travelled extensively in Italy and other parts of Europe, and he brought back rare specimens from European porcelain factories as well as a fine collection of china teacups, some tiny and with no handles from China. Chinese tea bowls were only about two and a quarter inches wide and between one and a half and two inches deep. They were not originally used with saucers, although the Chinese did develop a lacquered tray. The first matching saucers made for the European market were much smaller and deeper than modern-day saucers; they held the same amount of tea as the cup.

Date and Cinnamon Shortbread

Makes 16 fingers

12oz (350g) plain flour, sifted
1½ teaspoons ground cinnamon
9oz (250g) margarine, softened

6oz (175g) light soft brown sugar
6oz (175g) stoned dates, chopped small

Preheat the oven to gas mark 4/350°F/180°C. Grease an 11 × 7in (27·5 × 17·5cm) Swiss roll tin. Mix together the flour and cinnamon and rub in the margarine. Add the sugar and dates and stir well. Turn into the prepared tin and press down, smoothing the top with a palette knife. Bake for 30 minutes until golden. Remove from the oven and leave to cool in the tin. When cold, cut into fingers and lift carefully from the tin.

A Cider Tea, clockwise from top right: cider loaf (page 28); spicy apple flan (page 76); Gloucester apple shortbread (page 94).

Traditional Christmas Cake

Makes 1 × 8in (20cm) square cake or 1 × 9in (22·5cm) round cake

FOR THE CAKE
8oz (225g) currants
8oz (225g) sultanas
8oz (225g) raisins
4oz (100g) glacé cherries, chopped
½ glass brandy and port mixed together
1 teaspoon vanilla essence
1 teaspoon almond essence

8oz (225g) butter or margarine, softened
8oz (225g) light or dark soft brown sugar
4 large eggs, separated
8oz (225g) self-raising flour, sifted
1 teaspoon baking powder
1 teaspoon mixed spice

FOR THE DECORATION
8oz (225g) apricot jam
2–3 tablespoons water

1¼ lb (550g) marzipan

FOR THE ROYAL ICING
3 egg whites
1½ lb (675g) icing sugar, sifted

1 tablespoon lemon juice
1 teaspoon glycerine

Place the dried fruit, cherries, brandy and port, vanilla essence and almond essence in a bowl and leave to soak overnight. The next day preheat the oven to gas mark 2/300°F/150°C. Grease and line an 8in (20cm) square tin or a 9in (22·5cm) round tin. Beat together the butter or margarine and sugar. Beat the egg yolks and add with the fruit mixture to the fat and sugar, mixing well. Mix together the flour, baking powder and spice and add to the mixture. Stir thoroughly. Beat the egg whites until stiff and stir in. Turn into the prepared tin and bake for 2–2½ hours until a skewer comes out clean. Remove from oven and leave in tin for 30 minutes before turning out on to a wire rack to cool.

To decorate, heat the apricot jam and water in a small pan until the jam is dissolved. Push through a sieve and place in a clean pan. Bring back to the boil and simmer until fairly thick and smooth. Brush the mixture on to the outside of the cake. On a sugared surface, roll out two-thirds of the marzipan to form a rectangle as wide as the depth of the cake and twice as long. Place around the sides of the cake and press the ends well together. Roll out the remaining marzipan to make a circle to fit the top of the cake and put in place. Press the edges well together ensuring that the joins are neat. Leave in a warm room for 5–6 days until the marzipan has dried.

To make the icing, beat the egg whites until very frothy. Add half the icing sugar and beat in with a wooden spoon. Add the lemon juice, the glycerine and the remaining sugar and beat until the icing forms soft peaks. Cover with a damp cloth and leave in the bowl for a few hours to allow some of the air to escape. If the icing needs thickening, add a little more sugar as necessary.

Regional Specialities

Bath Buns

Makes 22 buns

FOR THE BUNS
1oz (25g) fresh yeast
4oz (100g) caster sugar
1lb 4oz (550g) strong plain white flour, sifted
5fl oz (150ml) milk, warmed
a pinch of salt

6oz (175g) currants and sultanas, mixed
2oz (50g) mixed candied peel
2oz (50g) butter, melted
2 eggs, beaten

FOR THE TOPPING
2oz (50g) lump sugar, coarsely crushed

In a medium-sized bowl, cream the yeast with 1 teaspoon of the sugar. Add 4oz (100g) of the flour and the warmed milk and mix to a thick batter. Leave in a warm place for 15-20 minutes until frothy. Mix together the remaining flour and the salt. Add the remaining caster sugar, currants, sultanas and peel. Add to the yeast mixture with the melted butter and most of the beaten egg (reserving a little for glazing) and mix to a soft dough. Knead on a floured board for 2–3 minutes until smooth. Place in a lightly floured bowl, cover with a damp cloth and leave in a warm place to rise for 1½–1¾ hours until doubled in size. Grease two baking trays. Knock back the dough and form into bun shapes, each weighing approximately 2½oz (65g). Place well apart on the prepared trays, cover with oiled cling film and leave to rise for about half an hour until doubled in size. Meanwhile heat the oven to gas mark 5/375°F/190°C. Glaze the buns with the remaining beaten egg and sprinkle with the crushed sugar. Bake for 15 minutes until well risen and golden. Remove from the oven and lift on to a wire rack to cool.

We had a kettle; we let it leak;
Our not repairing it made it worse.
We haven't had any tea for a week...
The bottom is out of the universe.

Rudyard Kipling (1865-1936), *Natural Theology*

Cornish Black Cake

Makes 1 × 8in (20cm) round cake

6oz (175g) butter, softened
6oz (175g) caster sugar
3–4 eggs, beaten
4oz (100g) plain flour, sifted
4oz (100g) ground rice
½ teaspoon mixed spice
¼ teaspoon grated nutmeg
½ teaspoon ground cinnamon
½ teaspoon baking powder

½ teaspoon bicarbonate of soda
1lb (450g) currants
4oz (100g) mixed candied peel
2oz (50g) sultanas
2oz (50g) raisins
3oz (75g) almonds, blanched and
    chopped
1 tablespoon brandy
a little milk for mixing

Preheat the oven to gas mark 3/325°F/170°C. Grease and line an 8in (20cm) round tin. Beat together the butter and sugar until light and fluffy. Add the eggs, flour, ground rice, spices, baking powder, bicarbonate of soda, dried fruit, nuts and brandy and mix carefully until all the ingredients are evenly distributed. If necessary add a little milk to give a soft mixture. Turn into the prepared tin, smooth the top and bake for 1 hour. Reduce the oven temperature to gas mark 1/275°F/140°C and cook for a further 1–1½ hours until a skewer comes out clean. Remove from the oven and leave to cool in the tin for 15 minutes, then turn out on to a wire rack to cool completely.

Devon Flats

Makes 24 flats

8oz (225g) self-raising flour,
    sifted
a pinch of salt
4oz (100g) caster sugar

4fl oz (100ml) clotted or double
    cream
1 egg, beaten
1 tablespoon fresh milk

Preheat the oven to gas mark 7/425°F/220°C. Grease two baking trays. Mix together the flour, salt and sugar. Add the cream, beaten egg and enough milk to give a stiff dough. On a lightly floured board, roll out to a thickness of approximately ⅜in (0·75cm) and cut into circles using a 3in (7·5cm) cutter. Place on the prepared trays and bake for 8–10 minutes until golden. Remove from the oven and lift carefully on to a wire rack to cool.

Wangyucheng of the Sung Dynasty wrote:
'Drink tea that your mind may be lively and clear.'

Heavy Cake

Makes 1 × 7in (17·5cm) flat, round cake

3oz (75g) lard, softened
6oz (175g) plain flour, sifted
a pinch of salt
1½ oz (40g) caster, granulated or demerara sugar

3oz (75g) currants
1oz (25g) mixed candied peel (optional)
a little cold water

Preheat the oven to gas mark 5/375°F/190°C. Grease a baking tray. Chop the lard roughly into small pieces. Mix the flour with the salt and stir the lard roughly in with a knife blade. Add the sugar, currants and peel and mix with enough cold water to give a stiff dough. On a floured board, roll out the dough to a flat round approximately 7in (17·5cm) in diameter. Place on the prepared tray and mark a diamond criss-cross pattern on the top with a knife blade. Bake for 25-30 minutes until golden brown. Serve warm, split and buttered.

This traditional Cornish cake was made in the southern part of the county, south of Truro, in fishing villages where 'seine' fishing took place. The seine net is a large, vertical net, the ends of which are brought together and hauled from the water. When the seine was being hauled in, the men shouted 'hevva' (or heave) with every pull. The womenfolk knew when they heard the sound that the men would soon arrive for their tea, so they quickly made this flat cake. The diamond criss-cross pattern represents the nets.

Sally Lunns

Makes 1 large flat cake or 5-6 small round cakes

1oz (25g) fresh yeast
2 teaspoons caster sugar
2 eggs, beaten
10fl oz (300ml) double cream

1lb (450g) plain flour, sifted
a pinch of salt
warm water for mixing

Cream together the yeast and sugar and mix with the beaten eggs and cream. Mix together the flour and salt. Add the yeast mixture and mix with enough warm water to give a light dough. Leave in the bowl in a warm place for 1½ hours until doubled in size. Grease a baking tray. Turn the dough on to a floured board and knead lightly. Shape into one large flat cake or five or six small ones and place on the tray. Leave in a warm place for a further 20-30 minutes until well risen. Meanwhile heat the oven to gas mark 6/400°F/200°C. When the cakes are well risen, bake for 20-25 minutes until golden. Remove from the oven, tear open and spread with thick cream or butter. Put back together and serve immediately.

The South-East

Many of the traditional recipes from the south of England have disappeared because of the strong influence on cookery from the Continent, but a few have survived against all odds and continue to be baked. Originally made and sold in the Old Chelsea Bun House in Pimlico by Richard Hand, known as Captain Bun, London's Chelsea buns are popular all over the country today. Surrey's Maids of Honour started life at Hampton Court in the days of Henry VIII. According to legend, one day he came across some of Anne Boleyn's maids enjoying some little tartlets, whereupon he asked to try one and declared that they were so good they should be made only for royal consumption. In George I's reign a lady of the court is supposed to have given the secret recipe to a gentleman who set up shop in Richmond. The recipe was made public in 1951.

Kent was once famous for its flead cakes which were rich, crisp and flaky cakes made with pigs' flead (the fat left after rendering the lard when the family pig had been killed). The flead was beaten into the dough with a wooden hoop; it was important that it was rolled out only once, as otherwise it became like pie crust rather than rising to twice its height during the cooking. Although flead cakes were notoriously difficult to make successfully, Kentish huffkins are easy to prepare and are delicious served with cooked cherries or apples from the Kent orchards. Huffkins are a soft white roll with a hole in the middle into which stewed fruit was traditionally piled just before serving. They would have been carried out to the hop fields to feed the bands of seasonal pickers from the East End of London who arrived each year for their annual working holiday.

BATEMAN'S

Bateman's is a modest Jacobean house of local sandstone which, according to tradition, was built by a Sussex ironmaster. Rudyard Kipling bought the house in 1902 when he was thirty-six. He once described Bateman's as standing 'like a beautiful cup on a saucer to match'. The heart of the house is the book-lined study at the top of the stairs; it was here that Kipling wrote some of his greatest works, including *Puck of Pook's Hill*, called after the hill visible from Bateman's, *If* and *The Glory of the Garden*. For these he drew his material from the Kent and Sussex countryside, no longer looking east to the India of his childhood for inspiration. None the less, the house also reflects his strong links with the subcontinent, with Oriental rugs in many of the rooms and Kipling's large collection of Indian artefacts and works of art displayed in the parlour.

The tradition of afternoon tea was firmly established at Bateman's by the Kiplings. They habitually took tea in the comfortable entrance hall, with its welcoming oak benches and its huge fireplace which burns five-foot logs. Tea was always served on a large Benares brass tray that was a wedding present from Kipling's sister, Alice.

In the grounds stands an old watermill that dates back to 1196. Kipling removed the waterwheel and installed a turbine which provided electricity for the house. The mill was renovated in 1976 and is now used, at least once a week, to grind the wheat grown on the estate.

Bateman's Soda Bread

Makes 1 × 6in (15cm) round loaf

8oz (225g) plain wholemeal flour, sifted
2 teaspoons baking powder
½ teaspoon salt
1 teaspoon demerara sugar

1oz (25g) margarine, softened
5fl oz (150ml) milk
cracked wheat, oatmeal or oats for sprinkling on top

Preheat the oven to gas mark 6/400°F/200°C. Grease a baking tray. Mix together the flour, baking powder, salt and sugar and rub in the margarine. Add the milk and mix to a soft dough. Shape into a round and place on the prepared tray. Brush the top with a little milk and sprinkle with cracked wheat, oatmeal or oats. Bake for 20–30 minutes until well risen and browned. Remove from the oven and serve warm with butter.

Orange Gingerbread

Makes 12 pieces

4oz (100g) margarine
4oz (100g) black treacle
4oz (100g) golden syrup
2oz (50g) light or dark soft brown sugar
1 teaspoon bicarbonate of soda
5fl oz (150ml) orange juice

8oz (225g) plain wholemeal flour, sifted
1 heaped teaspoon mixed spice
2 heaped teaspoons ground ginger
2 eggs, beaten
1½oz (40g) flaked almonds to decorate

Preheat the oven to gas mark 2/300°F/150°C. Grease and line a 7 × 11in (17·5 × 27·5cm) Swiss roll tin. In a medium-sized pan melt together the margarine, treacle, syrup and sugar over a low heat. Dissolve the bicarbonate of soda in the orange juice and add to the mixture. Stir well. Add the flour, spice, ginger and beaten eggs and beat well to a smooth batter. Pour into the prepared tin and scatter the flaked almonds over the top. Bake for 1 hour until firm and well risen. Remove from the oven and leave to cool in the tin. When cold, cut into bars and lift carefully from the tin.

Wholemeal Shortbread

Makes 16 fingers

5oz (150g) plain wholemeal flour, sifted
5oz (150g) plain white flour, sifted
5oz (150g) ground semolina
5oz (150g) demerara sugar
10oz (275g) slightly salted butter, softened
a little demerara sugar for sprinkling on top

Preheat the oven to gas mark 2/300°F/150°C. Grease an 11 × 7in (27·5 × 17·5cm) Swiss roll tin. Mix together the dry ingredients. Cut the butter into small pieces and rub into the flour with the fingertips. Work the mixture together to form a soft dough. Press into the prepared tin, smooth the top and prick all over with a fork. Bake for 1 hour 20 minutes until pale golden. Remove from the oven and sprinkle the demerara sugar over the top. Leave to cool in the tin for about 10 minutes. Using a sharp knife, cut into fingers and leave in the tin to finish cooling.

BOX HILL

It is the dramatic beauty of the 400-foot escarpment of the North Downs, where the River Mole has cut through the hills on its way to the Thames, which has brought visitors here ever since an eye for landscape began to be cultivated in the eighteenth century. The chalk downland and the woods make excellent countryside for long walks, and an added bonus is the breathtaking view over the South Downs. Box Hill takes its name from the steep chalk slopes, clothed in places with box, which John Evelyn noted in 1655. The shrub box (*Buxus sempervirens*) is native here, one of only a handful of places where it grows wild in Britain.

A Garden Tea, clockwise from top left: herb bread (page 88); American zucchini cake (page 89); pineapple upside-down cake (page 39).

Apricot Almond Shortcake

Makes 1 × 9in (22·5cm) round cake

1lb (450g) self-raising flour, sifted
8oz (225g) butter, softened
8oz (225g) caster sugar
2 eggs, beaten
2 teaspoons lemon juice

10oz (275g) ready-to-use dried
apricots, roughly chopped
1 egg white, lightly beaten
2oz (50g) flaked almonds

Preheat the oven to gas mark 3/325°F/160°C. Grease a 9in (22·5cm) loose-bottomed round shallow flan tin. Rub the butter into the flour and stir in the sugar. Add the eggs and lemon juice and mix to a firm dough. Divide into two portions. On a piece of cling film, roll out half the dough to make a circle to fit the prepared tin. Invert so that the dough rests in the tin, remove the cling film and press the dough down into the tin so that it lines the base and sides. Spread the chopped apricots over the dough. On a piece of cling film, roll out the remaining half of the dough to make a circle to fit the top and invert on to the apricots. Press the edges well together, brush the top with the beaten egg white and sprinkle with the flaked almonds. Bake for 45 minutes to 1 hour until golden. Remove from the oven and leave to cool in the tin. When cold, remove from the tin and cut into portions.

Banana and Pineapple Cake

Makes 1 × 9in (22·5cm) ring cake

5 or 6 tinned pineapple rings
7oz (200g) plain flour, sifted
1 teaspoon ground cinnamon
½ teaspoon bicarbonate of soda
7oz (200g) caster sugar
4oz (100g) pecans or walnuts,
roughly chopped

2 bananas, mashed
1 × 15¼oz (432g) can of crushed
pineapple, drained
4fl oz (100ml) corn or sunflower oil
2 eggs

Preheat the oven to gas mark 4/350°F/180°C. Grease and line a 9in (22·5cm) ring tin and place the pineapple rings in the base of the tin. Mix together all the other ingredients and spoon into the tin. Bake for 30–35 minutes until a skewer comes out clean. Remove from the oven and leave to cool in the tin. When cold, turn out and peel off the greaseproof paper. Serve with the pineapple rings uppermost.

A Welsh Tea, clockwise from top left: bara brith (pages 125–6);
Welsh cheese and herb scones (page 127); Welsh lardy cake (page 131).

Box Hill Bread Pudding

Makes 16 slabs

1lb (450g) bread (white, brown or a mixture)
8oz (225g) raisins or currants
4oz (100g) glacé cherries, cut in halves
4oz (100g) shredded suet

4oz (100g) caster sugar
2 teaspoons grated nutmeg
1 teaspoon ground cinnamon
2 eggs, beaten
milk for mixing

Break the bread into small pieces, cover with cold water and leave to soak for at least 1 hour. Preheat the oven to gas mark 3/325°F/160°C. Grease a shallow baking tin approximately 12 × 8in (30 × 20cm). Strain and squeeze as much water as possible out of the bread and beat to break up any lumps. Add the dried fruit, cherries, suet, sugar, spices and eggs and beat together, adding enough milk to give a soft, dropping consistency. Pour into the prepared tin and bake for 1½–2 hours until firm. Remove from the oven and leave to cool in the tin. When cold, cut into slabs.

This traditional cake is adapted from Mrs Beeton's original recipe.

CLANDON PARK

Clandon looks as if it would be more at home on the corner of a piazza in Venice or Florence than set in the Surrey countryside. This individual Georgian country house, built in about 1731, owes its appearance to the Italian Giacomo Leoni and is one of only five surviving buildings by this Venetian architect in England. Clandon was built for Thomas, 2nd Baron Onslow, to replace the Elizabethan house his grandfather had acquired in 1641, and it has remained in the family ever since. Thomas married a rich heiress, Elizabeth Knight, whose fortune from sugar plantations in Jamaica helped to create Clandon as it stands today. After the death of his first wife, a later Tom Onslow, the elder son of the 4th Baron, married Charlotte Duncombe, a lady-in-waiting to Queen Charlotte. She was a great favourite with the Queen who gave her two Dresden tea services. The small, delicate cups which sit on deep saucers are gold-edged and decorated with tiny pink and purple flowers.

The house also has a strong link with Queen Catharine, wife of Charles II. When Catharine of Braganza married Charles, her dowry included not only a chest of tea but also the Port of Tangier. A regiment was raised to garrison the new possession; originally called the First Tangier Regiment, it was later renamed the Queen's Royal Regiment. Today it is known as the Queen's Royal Surrey Regiment and its museum is in the basement of the house.

Orange and Lemon Cake

Makes 1 × 8in (20cm) round cake

8oz (225g) butter, softened
8oz (225g) caster sugar
3 eggs

the juice and rind of half an orange
the juice and rind of half a lemon
8oz (225g) plain flour, sifted

Preheat the oven to gas mark 3/325°F/160°C. Grease and line an 8in (20cm) round tin. Beat together the butter and sugar until light and fluffy. Add the eggs, orange and lemon rind and juice and beat well. Add the flour and beat carefully for a few seconds. Turn into the prepared tin and bake for 1 hour until a skewer comes out clean. Remove from the oven and leave to cool in the tin.

If liked, split in half and fill with butter filling made with the grated rind and juice from half a lemon and half an orange, 2oz (50g) softened butter and 6oz (175g) icing sugar, sifted. Decorate the top by dredging with icing sugar or spread with glacé icing made by mixing together 6oz (175g) icing sugar and the juice and grated rind of half a lemon and half an orange.

Spice Cake

Makes 1 × 8in (20cm) square cake

1lb (450g) plain flour, sifted
4 teaspoons mixed spice
a pinch of salt
8oz (225g) Trex or similar white
  shortening, softened
6oz (175g) caster sugar
6oz (175g) sultanas

6oz (175g) currants
10fl oz (300ml) milk
2 teaspoons white wine vinegar
2 teaspoons bicarbonate of soda
2 tablespoons demerara sugar for
  sprinkling

Preheat the oven to gas mark 3/325°F/160°C. Grease and line an 8in (20cm) square tin. Mix together the flour, spice and salt and rub in the fat. Add the caster sugar and dried fruit and mix well. Mix together the milk, vinegar and bicarbonate of soda and add to the mixture. Mix to a soft, fairly wet dough and turn into the prepared tin. Smooth the top and sprinkle with the demerara sugar. Bake for 1–1¼ hours until a skewer comes out clean. Remove from the oven and leave to cool in the tin.

Retired to their tea and scandal, according to their ancient custom.

William Congreve (1772-1828), *The Double Dealer*

CLAREMONT

The garden at Claremont was amongst the most famous in Europe in the eighteenth century. It is the product of some of the greatest names in garden history – Charles Bridgeman, Capability Brown and William Kent – and one of the first and finest gardens to be designed in the natural manner.

Laid out round a little lake on an undulating fifty-acre site, Claremont is primarily a study in foliage, grass and water, where the overall effect is created by contrasts of light and shade, by the alternation of open glades with densely wooded serpentine paths and by little buildings and other features set as eyecatchers at strategic points. Bordering the lake is an extraordinary turf amphitheatre, one of only two on such a scale in Europe, and a pavilion crowning the island in the lake once served as a summer-house.

In the eighteenth century it was fashionable to make excursions to summer-houses and pavilions in the vast grounds of stately homes to enjoy a picnic or a tea party. Servants would be included in the number so that they could prepare and serve the food in as elegant a way as possible. Claremont's pavilion was originally used for fishing parties, but must also have provided the perfect setting for afternoon tea.

Flapjack

Makes 12 pieces

4oz (100g) margarine
4 tablespoons golden syrup

3oz (75g) self-raising wholemeal flour, sifted
8oz (225g) rolled oats

Preheat the oven to gas mark 3/325°F/160°C. Grease a shallow 7½in (18cm) square tin. In a medium-sized pan, melt the margarine and syrup over a low heat. Remove from the heat and add the flour and oats. Mix thoroughly so that all the ingredients are evenly distributed. Turn into the prepared tin, press down and smooth the top with a palette knife. Bake for 30–40 minutes until golden. Remove from the oven and leave to cool in the tin for 5–10 minutes, then cut into pieces and lift carefully on to a wire rack to finish cooling.

Sue's Amazing Cheese Scones

Makes 14-16 scones

FOR THE SCONES
1lb (450g) self-raising white or wholewheat flour, or a mixture of half and half, sifted
2 teaspoons baking powder
4oz (100g) margarine, softened
1 egg
2 dessertspoons natural yogurt

approximately 15fl oz (400ml) milk
a large pinch of dry English mustard powder
4oz (100g) strong Cheddar cheese, grated

FOR THE TOPPING
a little milk
1oz (25g) strong Cheddar cheese, grated

Preheat the oven to gas mark 6/400°F/200°C. Grease a large baking tray. Mix together the flour and baking powder and rub in the fat. In a pint measure, beat together the egg and yogurt and make up to just under 1 pint (600ml) with milk. Mix well. Add the mustard and cheese. Make a well in the flour and add the milk and cheese mixture. Mix carefully to a very soft dough and, if too wet to roll, add a little more flour. On a well-floured board, roll out the dough to a thickness of ¾in (1·5cm) and cut into rounds using a 2½in (6cm) cutter. Place on the prepared baking tray and brush the tops with milk. Sprinkle with a little more cheese and bake for 15-20 minutes until golden. Remove from the oven and lift on to a wire rack to cool. Serve with butter and cheese.

Sue's Amazing Rock Cakes

Makes 12 cakes

8oz (225g) plain wholewheat flour, sifted
4oz (100g) plain white flour, sifted
4 teaspoons baking powder
1 teaspoon mixed spice
1 teaspoon grated nutmeg

6oz (175g) margarine, softened
3oz (75g) light soft brown sugar
6oz (175g) mixed dried fruit
1 egg, beaten
a little milk for mixing
caster sugar for dredging

Preheat the oven to gas mark 7/425°F/220°C. Grease a large baking tray. Mix together the flour, baking powder and spices. Rub in the fat then stir in the sugar and dried fruit. Add the beaten egg and enough milk to mix to a stiff dough. Spoon on to the prepared tray and bake for 15-20 minutes until golden. Remove from the oven and dredge with caster sugar. Serve warm with butter.

PETWORTH

The park at Petworth is considered to be Capability Brown's masterpiece, one of the greatest man-made landscapes created in eighteenth-century Europe. Brown's sublime landscape encloses Petworth House, a magnificent late seventeenth-century baroque palace filled with an exceptional collection of works of art, including furniture, *objets d'art*, books and sculpture as well as paintings by Turner, Van Dyck, Reynolds and Holbein.

The porcelain is also notable. The huge vases in the staircase hall were probably collected by the Duchess of Somerset in the late seventeenth and early eighteenth century. She is known to have had a passion for Oriental porcelain and had a 'china closet' in her apartments. In this she would almost certainly have displayed tea ware, mostly at that time from China. In the early days of tea drinking, teapots and teacups were imported; it was at this stage that the word 'china' entered the English language to encompass all the wares that were arriving from the Orient. Chinese teacups were tiny, holding only a tablespoon or two of tea, and had no handles. The idea of the handle developed from the English posset cup which was used for drinking hot mulled wines and ales.

Almond-Topped Apricot Cake

Makes 1 × 9in (22·5cm) round cake

FOR THE CAKE
6oz (175g) butter, softened
6oz (175g) caster sugar
3 eggs
6oz (175g) self-raising flour, sifted

3oz (75g) ground almonds
4oz (100g) ready-to-use dried
   apricots, chopped

FOR THE TOPPING
2oz (50g) butter
2oz (50g) demerara sugar

1 tablespoon golden syrup
2oz (50g) flaked almonds

Preheat the oven to gas mark 4/350°F/180°C. Grease and base-line a 9in (22·5cm) loose-bottomed round tin. Beat together the butter and sugar until light and fluffy. Beat in the eggs one at a time, adding a tablespoon of flour with each. Fold in the remaining flour, the ground almonds and the apricots and mix well. Turn into the prepared tin and bake for 40 minutes. Meanwhile prepare the topping. In a small pan mix together the butter, sugar and syrup and heat gently until the sugar dissolves. Remove from the heat and stir in the almonds. When the 40 minutes' cooking time is up, remove the cake from the oven and spoon the topping over. Return to the oven and bake for a further 10–15 minutes until golden brown. Remove from the oven and leave to cool in the tin.

Petworth Pudding

Makes 16 fingers

4oz (100g) butter or margarine
4oz (100g) granulated or caster
  sugar
1oz (25g) cocoa powder, sifted
1 egg
8oz (225g) digestive biscuits,
  crushed

2oz (50g) raisins or sultanas
2oz (50g) dark chocolate
2oz (50g) walnuts, chopped,
  or 2oz (50g) shredded coconut
2oz (50g) glacé cherries, roughly
  chopped

Grease a 7 × 11in (17·5 × 27·5cm) Swiss roll tin. Melt the butter or margarine and sugar in a medium-sized pan. Beat in the cocoa powder and the egg. Stir in the crushed biscuits and raisins or sultanas and turn into the prepared tin. Press down well and smooth the top with a palette knife. Melt the chocolate and pour over the top. Mix together the walnuts or coconut and cherries and sprinkle over the chocolate. Place the tin in the refrigerator and leave to set. When cold, cut into fingers.

The recipe for this wonderfully rich cake was found in the house archives. It is good served as a cake, but it also makes an excellent dessert.

Sussex Apple Cake

Makes 1 × 9in (22·5cm) round cake

8oz (225g) margarine, softened
8oz (225g) dark soft brown sugar
3 large eggs
5oz (150g) walnuts, finely chopped
  or crushed
5oz (150g) sultanas or raisins

8oz (225g) wholemeal self-raising
  flour, sifted
14oz (400g) cooking apples, peeled,
  cored and grated
½ teaspoon ground cloves

Preheat the oven to gas mark 4/350°F/180°C. Grease and base-line a 9in (22·5cm) loose-bottomed round tin. Beat together the margarine and 6oz (175g) of the sugar until light and fluffy. Add the eggs and beat hard. Fold in 4oz (100g) of the walnuts, the sultanas or raisins and the flour, mixing well so that all the ingredients are evenly distributed. Put half the mixture into the prepared tin. Mix together the apples and cloves and spread over the layer of cake mixture. Spread the remaining cake mixture on top and smooth with a palette knife. Mix together the remaining sugar and walnuts and sprinkle evenly over the top of the cake. Bake for 1¼–1½ hours until the top is caramelised but not too brown. Remove from the oven and leave to cool in the tin.

POLESDEN LACEY

Polesden Lacey, a comfortable two-storey Regency villa, is alive with the spirit of Mrs Ronald Greville, captured so well in the vivacious and charming portrait which now greets visitors in the Picture Corridor. Those invited to the famous weekend parties held here from 1906 until the outbreak of the Second World War included Indian maharajahs, literary figures such as Beverley Nichols, Osbert Sitwell and Harold Nicolson, and prominent politicians of the day. Edward VII was a close friend of the elegant society hostess, and the future George VI and Queen Elizabeth were lent Polesden Lacey for part of their honeymoon in 1923.

Food and drink played a vital role in the social whirl of such a household, and Mrs Greville employed a French chef who was renowned for his high standards and his varied and interesting menus. Much of the produce was grown on the estate, and during the London season fruit, vegetables, flowers and dairy produce were sent daily from Polesden Lacey to the Grevilles' London house.

Tea-time was an integral part of life at Polesden Lacey. In *Down the Kitchen Sink* Beverley Nichols noted: 'Tea is at 5 o'clock – and not at 5 minutes past – which means that the Spanish ambassador, who has gone for a walk down the yew avenue, hastily retraces his steps, and that the Chancellor of the Exchequer … hurries down the great staircase, and that various gentlemen rise from their *chaises-longues* … and join the procession to the tea-room. The teapots, the cream jugs, the milk pots and the sugar basins are Queen Anne silver; the tea service is Meissen; and the doyleys, heavily monogrammed, are of Chantilly lace.'

Boodle Cake

Makes 1 × 9in (22·5cm) square cake

1lb (450g) plain flour, sifted
10oz (275g) butter, softened
10oz (275g) light soft brown or raw cane sugar
1lb (450g) raisins
2 eggs, beaten
10fl oz (300ml) milk

Preheat the oven to gas mark 3/325°F/160°C. Grease and line a 9in (22·5cm) square tin. Rub the butter into the flour until the mixture resembles breadcrumbs. Stir in the sugar and raisins. Add the eggs and milk and mix to a soft dough. Turn into the prepared tin, spread evenly with a palette knife and bake for 2 hours until a skewer comes out clean. Remove from the oven and turn out on to a wire rack to cool.

This recipe has seventeenth-century origins and makes a wonderful fruity cake.

Carrot Cake with Lime Topping

Makes 1 × 2lb (900g) loaf or 1 × 7in (17·5cm) round cake

FOR THE CAKE
2 eggs
4oz (100g) light soft brown sugar
3fl oz (75ml) oil (sunflower, safflower, vegetable or corn)

4oz (100g) self-raising flour, sifted
6oz (175g) grated carrot
1 teaspoon ground cinnamon
2oz (50g) shredded coconut

FOR THE TOPPING
6oz (175g) cream cheese
4oz (100g) icing sugar

the grated rind and juice of 1 lime

Preheat the oven to gas mark 5/375°F/190°C. Grease and line a 2lb (900g) loaf tin or a 7in (17·5cm) round tin. Beat together the eggs and sugar until very creamy. Add the oil and beat hard. Fold in the remaining ingredients and turn into the prepared tin. Smooth the top then slightly hollow out the middle. Bake for 1 hour until golden and well risen and a skewer comes out clean. Remove from the oven and turn out on to a wire rack to cool. To make the topping, beat the ingredients together until light and creamy and spread over the top of the cake. Make a pattern with the prongs of a fork.

Secretary Tarts

Makes 24 tarts

1lb (450g) rich shortcrust or shortcrust pastry (see page 16)
6oz (175g) butter
6oz (175g) light soft brown sugar

1 large can (14oz/405g) condensed milk
2oz (50g) walnuts, roughly chopped
2oz (50g) raisins

Make the pastry according to the instructions on page 16 and chill for at least 15 minutes. Preheat the oven to gas mark 8/450°F/230°C. Grease twenty-four patty tins. On a floured board, roll out the pastry to a thickness of ¼in (0·5cm) and cut twenty-four circles using a 3in (7·5cm) fluted cutter. Use to line the prepared patty tins. Place little squares of greaseproof paper in each tart and fill with baking beans. Bake blind for 10 minutes. Remove from the oven, lift the baking beans and paper out of the cases and return to the oven for a further 5 minutes. Remove and switch off the oven. Put the butter, sugar and milk into a medium-sized pan and bring to the boil. Boil hard for 7 minutes, stirring all the time, until the mixture becomes a caramel colour. Remove from the heat and allow to cool for 5 minutes. Stir in the walnuts and raisins and spoon into the pastry cases. Put into the refrigerator to set.

SISSINGHURST

The beauty and charm of this exceptional garden set high on a ridge above the Vale of Kent owe much to the Tudor buildings around which it was created and which form a romantic backdrop to the planting. The focal point of the garden is a four-storey red-brick Elizabethan prospect tower with two octagonal turrets, a remnant of the great mansion built by Sir Richard Baker in the mid-sixteenth century. Despite over 200 years of neglect and decay, these romantic remains inspired the novelist and biographer Vita Sackville-West to purchase the property in 1930 and with the help of her husband, Sir Harold Nicolson, the diplomat and literary critic, to create one of the greatest gardens of the twentieth century. Nigel Nicolson, their son, recalled his first visit here in *Portrait of a Marriage*: 'It was the battered relic of an Elizabethan house in which not a single room was habitable. The future garden was a rubbish dump.' Nothing daunted, Vita reacted by saying: 'I think we shall be very happy here . . . yes, I think we can make something rather lovely out of it.'

One of the best places to appreciate Sissinghurst is from the top of the tower, reached by a spiral staircase which leads up past the cluttered room where Vita Sackville-West wrote, its walls lined with books reflecting her special interests – gardening, literature, history and travel. Beyond the borders of the garden, the tower looks out over woods, fields and oasthouses to a distant ridge of the North Downs.

Kentish Hop Pickers' Cake

Makes 1 × 2lb (900g) loaf

10oz (275g) self-raising flour, sifted
1 teaspoon ground ginger
1 teaspoon mixed spice
6oz (175g) margarine, softened
4oz (100g) light soft brown sugar
4oz (100g) sultanas
4oz (100g) currants
2oz (50g) mixed candied peel
15fl oz (400ml) milk
1 tablespoon black treacle
½ teaspoon bicarbonate of soda
1 teaspoon cream of tartar

Preheat the oven to gas mark 3/325°F/160°C. Grease and line a 2lb (900g) loaf tin. Mix together the flour, ginger and spice and rub in the margarine. Add the sugar and dried fruit and mix well. Warm the milk and treacle together and add the bicarbonate of soda and cream of tartar. Gradually add to the flour mixture and beat well. Pour into the prepared tin and bake for 1½ hours until a skewer comes out clean. Remove from the oven and turn out on to a wire rack to cool.

Kentish Pudding Pies

Makes 24 tarts

1lb (450g) shortcrust pastry
  (see page 16)
3 strips of lemon peel
1 pint (600ml) milk
4oz (100g) butter
3oz (75g) caster sugar

2 eggs, beaten
2oz (50g) ground rice
a pinch of salt
the juice of half a lemon
2oz (50g) currants

Make the pastry according to the instructions on page 16 and chill for 15 minutes. Put the milk and lemon peel in a pan and stand it over a gentle heat for about 20 minutes. Meanwhile preheat the oven to gas mark 4/350°F/180°C. Grease twenty-four patty tins. On a floured board, roll out the pastry to a thickness of ¼in (0·5cm) and cut twenty-four circles using a 3in (7·5cm) cutter. Line the prepared patty tins with the pastry circles. Remove the strips of lemon peel from the milk and discard. Add the butter and 2oz (50g) of the sugar to the milk and stir well. Mix together the beaten eggs, the ground rice, salt and lemon juice and add to the saucepan. Stir over a gentle heat until the mixture begins to thicken. Stir in the currants. Spoon the mixture into the pastry cases and sprinkle with the remaining sugar. Bake for 25-30 minutes until the pastry is golden and the filling is firm and well risen. Remove from the oven and leave to cool in the tins.

These little tarts are typical of the cheesecakes and egg custards that were popular in England as far back as the seventeenth century. Until the nineteenth century, eggs, like all animal products, were forbidden during the Lenten fast. The hens of course went on laying during Lent, and the surplus of eggs was used over the Easter weekend in egg custards and tarts. In Kent these would be eaten with cherry beer – ale with cherry juice added.

STANDEN

Standen is a most unusual house, built in 1892-4 and yet not at all Victorian, designed all of a piece and yet seeming to have grown out of the group of old farm buildings to which it is attached. This peaceful place on the edge of the Weald was designed by Philip Webb for the successful London solicitor James Beale, who wanted a roomy house for his large family for weekends and holidays. A life-long friend and associate of William Morris, Webb shared Morris's views on the value of high-quality materials and craftsmanship.

The rooms are light and airy, furnished with Morris's wallpapers and textiles, with richly coloured William de Morgan pottery, such as the ochre-red ware in a cabinet in the drawing-room, and with a pleasing mixture of antiques and beautifully made pieces from Morris's company. Tea was evidently an important part of life at Standen: a Rockingham service by T. E. Colcutt is displayed in the morning-room and a silver muffin dish by Ashbee, which could have been used at breakfast or tea, is on show in the dining-room. An inventory in the kitchen records that Dundee cake at 3s. 0d. and almond cake at 3s. 6d. were ordered from W. & G. Buzzard of Oxford Street in 1910, and that chocolate macaroons and praline macaroons cost 2s. 0d. (presumably for a dozen).

A Japanese tea service on show in the drawing-room is a reminder that tea drinking took root in Japan in the seventh century and that early European traders imported both Chinese and Japanese teas to Holland and Portugal during the first half of the seventeenth century. Japanese tea ware also found its way from the Orient and eventually became popular in Britain. The Japanese tea ceremony evolved from the rituals of Zen Buddhism; it can last for up to four hours, with strictly defined periods of welcome, preparation, meditation, communal tea drinking, conversation and individual tea drinking.

Raisin and Bran Bread

Makes 1 × 2lb (900g) loaf

3oz (75g) bran cereal (All Bran or similar)
3oz (75g) sugar
6oz (175g) raisins
10fl oz (300ml) milk

6oz (175g) wholemeal self-raising flour, sifted
2-3fl oz (50-75ml) milk and water mixed in equal measures

Put the bran cereal, sugar, raisins and milk into a bowl and leave overnight (or for at least 6 hours), stirring occasionally. Preheat the oven to gas mark 3/325°F/160°C. Grease and line a 2lb (900g) loaf tin. Add the flour to the soaked ingredients and mix with enough of the milk and water to give a runny consistency. Pour into the prepared tin and bake for 1 hour. Remove from the oven and leave to cool in the tin.

The bran gives this bread a pleasant, rather coarse texture. It contains very little fat and sugar and is therefore ideal for anybody who is concerned about cholesterol or calories.

Love and scandal are the best sweeteners of tea.

Henry Fielding (1707-54), *Love in Several Masques*

Wholemeal Coconut Loaf

Makes 1 × 2lb (900g) loaf or 1 × 7in (17·5cm) round cake

4oz (100g) margarine, softened
8oz (225g) self-raising wholemeal flour, sifted
4oz (100g) caster sugar

4oz (100g) finely shredded coconut
4fl oz (100ml) milk
2 eggs

Preheat the oven to gas mark 4/350°F/180°C. Grease and line a 2lb (900g) loaf tin or a 7in (17·5cm) round tin. Rub the margarine into the flour. Stir in the sugar and coconut. Beat together the milk and eggs and stir into the mixture to give a soft, dropping consistency. Turn into the prepared tin and bake for 45–50 minutes until a skewer comes out clean. Remove from the oven and turn on to a wire rack to cool.

Regional Specialities

Chelsea Buns

Makes 9 buns

8oz (225g) strong plain white flour, sifted
½oz (15g) fresh yeast
1 teaspoon caster sugar
4fl oz (100g) warm milk
½oz (15g) lard, softened
a pinch of salt
1 egg, beaten

2oz (50g) butter or margarine, melted
2oz (50g) raisins
2oz (50g) currants
2oz (50g) sultanas
1oz (25g) mixed candied peel
2oz (50g) light soft brown sugar
honey to glaze

Grease a 7in (17·5cm) square tin. Put 2oz (50g) of the flour into a bowl and add the yeast, caster sugar and milk. Mix to a smooth batter and leave in a warm place for 20 minutes until frothy. Rub the lard into the remaining flour. Add the salt, the yeast mixture and the beaten egg, and mix to a soft dough. Knead on a floured board for about 5 minutes until really smooth. Place in a bowl, cover with a clean, damp cloth and leave in a warm place for 1–1½ hours until doubled in size. Knead again on a floured board and then roll out to a rectangle approximately 12 × 9in (30 × 22·5cm). Brush the melted butter over the surface and sprinkle the dried fruit and sugar over, leaving a narrow border all the way round the edge. Roll up like a Swiss roll, starting with the longer side. Brush the edges of the dough with water and seal carefully. Cut the roll into nine pieces and place the rolls, cut side uppermost, in the prepared tin. Leave in a warm place for a further 30 minutes until well risen. Meanwhile heat the oven to gas mark 5/375°F/190°C. When the buns are risen, bake for 30–35 minutes until golden. Remove from the oven, turn out on to a wire rack and, while still warm, brush the tops with honey. To serve, pull apart and eat warm or cold.

Kentish Huffkins

Makes 12 huffkins

1lb (450g) plain flour, sifted
½ teaspoon salt
1oz (25g) lard, softened
1oz (25g) fresh yeast

1 teaspoon caster sugar
12fl oz (350ml) milk, or a mixture
   of milk and water, warmed

Grease two baking trays. Sift together the flour and salt and rub in the lard. Cream the yeast with the sugar and add to the warmed milk (or milk and water). Add to the flour and mix to a light, soft dough. Leave in a warm place for about 1 hour until doubled in size. On a floured board, knead the dough lightly then divide into twelve flat oval cakes about ½in (1cm) thick. Place on the prepared trays and leave in a warm place for about 30 minutes until well risen. Meanwhile heat the oven to gas mark 6/400°F/200°C. When the huffkins are well risen, make a hole with the thumb in the middle of each and bake for 10-20 minutes until lightly browned and firm. Remove from the oven and cover immediately with a clean, dry cloth until cold; this helps to keep the rolls soft.

Maids of Honour

Makes approximately 24 tarts

1lb (450g) rich shortcrust pastry
   (see page 16)
4oz (100g) curd cheese
3oz (75g) butter, softened
2 eggs, beaten
2½fl oz (65ml) brandy

3oz (75g) caster sugar
3oz (75g) cold mashed potatoes
1oz (25g) ground almonds
½ teaspoon grated nutmeg
the grated rind of 2 lemons
the juice of 1 lemon

Make the pastry according to the instructions on page 16 and chill for at least 15 minutes. Preheat the oven to gas mark 4/350°F/180°C. Grease twenty-four patty tins. On a lightly floured board, roll out the pastry and cut twenty-four circles using a 3in (7·5cm) cutter. Use to line the prepared patty tins. Beat together the curd cheese and butter. Add the beaten eggs, brandy and sugar and beat again. In a separate bowl beat together the mashed potatoes, almonds, nutmeg, lemon rind and juice, and gradually mix in the cheese mixture. Beat thoroughly. Spoon into the pastry cases and bake for 35-40 minutes until risen, golden and firm. Remove from the oven and leave to cool in the tins for 5-10 minutes before lifting carefully on to a wire rack to finish cooling.

Eastern Counties

The first British saffron-growing estates were set up in Saffron Walden in Essex in the fourteenth century in order to provide cheap alternatives to imports. Production died out in the fifteenth century and subsequent supplies were shipped in from the East Indies with other herbs and spices. As many of the ships docked on the Cornish coast, saffron recipes can be found there rather than in the Eastern Counties. Like Cornwall and Devon, however, honey has been a local product here for hundreds of years, particularly at Walsingham in Norfolk where the monks in the priory kept colonies of bees. Honey cakes and buns are therefore a local speciality.

Lincolnshire is famous for its flat, gingerbread biscuits that were once baked for the annual fair at Grantham; Ashbourne in Derbyshire is known for its similar speciality. Norwich fairs also sold gingerbread husbands and wives, and the Cambridge fair always provided a good supply of gingerbreads and brandy snaps as well as nougat and rock. Many of the traditional cakes for this rural area have descended from the easily produced and filling cakes and breads that were carried out to the workers in the cornfields and apple orchards. The farmers' wives worked hard, especially during the harvest, to produce food for four or five meals a day for all the itinerant workers and regular labourers. Food, home-made lemonades and tea were transported in bags, baskets and jugs by the womenfolk and children for the midday and mid-afternoon meals. Everyone stopped work to enjoy the sociable gathering and a well-earned break.

Surely everyone is aware of the divine pleasures which attend
a wintry fireside: candles at four o'clock, warm hearthrugs,
tea, a fair tea-maker, shutters closed, curtains flowing in ample
draperies to the floor, whilst the wind and rain are raging
audibly without.

Thomas De Quincy (1785-1859), *Confessions of an English Opium-eater*

ANGLESEY ABBEY

Anglesey Abbey was an Augustinian religious house for almost 400 years from 1135 until the Dissolution of the Monasteries in 1535. It was then bought by Thomas Hobson, famous for the origin of the phrase 'Hobson's choice'. He was a Cambridge carrier who refused to let out any of his horses except in its turn, so Hobson's choice was the horse he offered or none at all. An interest in horse racing led Huttleston Broughton, later 1st Lord Fairhaven, to purchase Anglesey Abbey in 1926. A typical stone Jacobean manor house, it was conveniently placed for Newmarket and the stud he owned with his brother at Bury St Edmunds.

Over the next forty years this comfortable gentleman's residence was transformed. Although his sporting interests were never neglected, Lord Fairhaven devoted most of his fortune to the acquisition of an outstanding and wide-ranging collection of works of art, for which he adapted and extended the house. More remarkably, ninety acres of unpromising fen were used to create an imaginative and individual garden.

Inside the house there is a fascinating piece of Ming porcelain that started life as a ginger jar and was later converted into a teapot; about seven inches tall, it is made of brown clay slipware decorated with a creamy white design on each side. A delicate silver spout and handle have been added, a silver cherub stands on top of the lid and the jar sits on a fine silver mount. The date of the conversion is not known but it is certainly not later than the eighteenth century. The mount was probably made in Augsburg in Germany which was famous for its unique metalwork. The pot was originally part of the Burghley House Collection which was sold by Christie's in 1888. In 1910 it was exhibited at the Burlington Fine Arts Club by Lord Swaythling.

Applecake Fingers

Makes 15 pieces

FOR THE CAKE
5oz (150g) plain flour, sifted
5oz (150g) sugar
½ teaspoon baking powder
½ teaspoon mixed spice
a pinch of salt

3½oz (90g) margarine, softened
1 large egg, beaten
3fl oz (75ml) milk
2½oz (65g) cooking or eating
  apples, chopped

FOR THE GLAZE
6-8oz (175-225g) icing sugar,
  sifted
1½-2 tablespoons water

a few drops of lemon juice and a
  little grated lemon rind
  (optional)

Preheat the oven to gas mark 5/375°F/190°C. Grease a 7 × 11in (17·5 × 27·5cm) Swiss roll tin. Mix together the flour, sugar, baking powder, spice and salt and rub in the margarine until the mixture resembles fine breadcrumbs. Add the beaten egg and milk and mix until smooth. Add the chopped apple and mix so that it is evenly distributed. Press into the prepared tin and bake for approximately 35 minutes until golden and firm. Remove from the oven and leave to cool in the tin. When cold, mix together the icing sugar, water, lemon juice and rind if using, and pour the icing over the top of the cake. Leave to set, then cut the cake into fingers and lift carefully from the tin.

Ginger Bars

Makes 15 bars

FOR THE CAKE

12oz (350g) rich shortcrust or
    shortcrust pastry (see page 16)
2oz (50g) golden syrup
2oz (50g) black treacle
2½oz (65g) light or dark soft
    brown sugar
2oz (50g) white shortening
    (Trex or similar), melted

4fl oz (100ml) milk
5½oz (165g) plain flour, sifted
1 teaspoon ground ginger
½ teaspoon mixed spice
1 teaspoon bicarbonate of soda
a pinch of baking powder

FOR THE GLAZE

6–8oz (175–225g) icing sugar,
    sifted

1½–2 tablespoons water

Make the pastry according to the instructions on page 16 and chill for at least 15 minutes. Preheat the oven to gas mark 5/375°F/190°C. Grease a 7 × 11in (17·5 × 27·5cm) Swiss roll tin. On a lightly floured board, roll out the pastry and use to line the prepared tin. Mix together the syrup, treacle, sugar, melted fat and milk. Add the dry ingredients and mix thoroughly. Turn into the pastry case and smooth. Bake for approximately 30 minutes until firm and well risen. Remove from the oven and leave to cool in the tin. When cold, mix together the icing sugar and water and pour the icing over the top of the cake. Leave to set, then cut into bars and lift carefully from the tin.

BLICKLING HALL

Built of warm red brick with stone dressings, Robert Lyminge's Jacobean mansion for Sir Henry Hobart, James I's distinguished Chief Justice of the Common Pleas, looks confidently out at the world. The medieval manor which had fired Sir Henry's imagination – home of Anne Boleyn, Henry VIII's ill-fated second queen, and Sir John Fastolfe, inspiration for Shakespeare's tragic clown – has long disappeared, but its ghost lives on in the dry moat and in the layout of the courtyard house.

In the sunny kitchen there are two sugar cones on display with a pair of nippers. It is known that sugar was used in Britain before the days of the crusading knights, but it became more widely available after it began to be imported along with other spices and flavourings. Sugar was originally employed as a spice and sometimes as a medicine for colds. It first became popular as a sweetener in tea at the end of the seventeenth century, and sugar tongs, teaspoons and other accoutrements began to appear at about the same time. As sugar was so expensive, due to high taxes which continued until the nineteenth century, poorer folk often used large quantities of honey instead.

Stiffkey Cakes

Makes 8 cakes

12oz (350g) plain flour, sifted
1 teaspoon baking powder
1oz (25g) butter, softened
1oz (25g) caster sugar
2 eggs, beaten
a few drops of lemon essence or
    the juice of half a lemon
caster sugar for dredging

Preheat the oven to gas mark 6/400°F/200°C. Grease a baking tray. Mix together the flour and baking powder and rub in the fat. Add the sugar and mix well. Add the beaten eggs and lemon essence or juice and mix to a soft dough. On a floured board, roll out to a thickness of 1in (2·5cm) and cut into rounds using a 2½in (6cm) cutter. Place on the prepared tray and bake for 15 minutes until pale golden. Remove from the oven and lift carefully on to a wire rack to cool. Dredge with caster sugar before serving.

These cakes are rather like scones and were made in the 1860s by a local woman called Peggy Muns. Stiffkey on the north Norfolk coast is also famous for its dark shelled cockles, known as Stewkey Blues.

Walsingham Honey Cake

Makes 1 × 7in (17·5cm) square cake

FOR THE CAKE

8oz (225g) butter, softened
8oz (225g) light soft brown sugar
2 eggs, beaten
1lb (450g) plain flour, sifted
1 teaspoon ground ginger
1 teaspoon bicarbonate of soda

4oz (100g) raisins
2oz (50g) mixed candied peel
2oz (50g) glacé cherries, halved
10fl oz (300ml) milk
3oz (75g) clear honey
3oz (75g) black treacle

FOR THE TOPPING

3–4 tablespoons clear honey
1½ oz (40g) light soft brown sugar

2oz (50g) butter
2oz (50g) flaked almonds

Preheat the oven to gas mark 3/325°F/160°C. Grease and line a 7in (17·5cm) square tin. Beat together the butter and sugar until light and fluffy. Add the beaten eggs and beat again. Add the flour, ginger and bicarbonate of soda and beat well. Stir in the dried fruit and cherries. Warm together the milk, honey and treacle and add gradually, beating well and making sure that all the ingredients are evenly distributed. Turn into the prepared tin and bake for 2 hours until a skewer comes out clean. Remove from the oven and leave in the tin. Warm together the honey, sugar and butter and pour over the warm cake. Sprinkle with the almonds and allow to cool completely in the tin.

Little Walsingham became an important place of pilgrimage during medieval times after a vision of the Virgin Mary was seen there. The area has long been famous for its bees and honey; this is a traditional recipe from the town.

ICKWORTH

Frederick Augustus Hervey, 4th Earl of Bristol, must rank as one of the Church's more remarkable bishops. Appointed to the see of Derry, the richest in Ireland, in 1768 when only thirty-eight, his sympathy with both Roman Catholics and Presbyterians made him enormously popular. A large income coupled with an inherited fortune allowed him to embark on extensive foreign tours during which he amassed the works of art intended for display in his new house on the family's Suffolk estate.

Ickworth is as grandiose and flamboyant as its creator. A huge domed rotunda decorated with classical columns and terracotta friezes is linked by curving corridors to rectangular wings. Sadly, Frederick did not live to see his house completed, though his plans were realised by his son, created 1st Marquess of Bristol in 1826.

As well as some superb paintings and furniture, there is a fine display of silver and porcelain, including tea urns, sugar bowls and serving dishes. The basement of the central rotunda contains the domestic quarters – offices, kitchen, cellars, housekeeper's and butler's rooms and servants' hall – which are connected by underground corridors to the family's wing where there were also smaller kitchens. When there was a large house party to be catered for, presumably the entire household staff moved into the more roomy quarters in the rotunda.

Mincemeat Cake

Makes 1 × 8in (20cm) round cake

8oz (225g) self-raising flour, sifted
5oz (150g) margarine, softened
5oz (150g) light or dark soft brown sugar

3oz (75g) sultanas
1lb (450g) mincemeat
2 eggs, beaten
1–2oz (25–50g) flaked almonds

Preheat the oven to gas mark 3/325°F/160°C. Grease and line an 8in (20cm) round tin. Keeping aside the flaked almonds, put all the ingredients into a bowl and mix thoroughly. Turn into the prepared tin and sprinkle the flaked almonds over the top. Bake for 1¾ hours until a skewer comes out clean. Remove from the oven and leave in the tin for about 15 minutes before turning out on to a wire rack to cool completely.

Spicy Apple Flan

Makes 8 portions

FOR THE BASE
6oz (175g) self-raising flour, sifted
4oz (100g) margarine, softened
1 egg, beaten

1½ oz (40g) granulated or light or dark soft brown sugar
a pinch of salt

FOR THE TOPPING
5 large cooking apples, peeled, cored and sliced
2oz (50g) sugar

1 teaspoon mixed spice
2oz (50g) sultanas

Preheat the oven to gas mark 4/350°F/180°C. Grease a 7in (17·5cm) round tin. Using a fork or electric beater, mix together the ingredients for the base and, on a lightly floured board, roll out to make a circle to fit the tin. Place in the tin and press well against the edges. Arrange the apples in layers on top of the dough, sprinkling some of the sugar, spice and sultanas on each layer. Bake for 1 hour, watching carefully, until the top is browned and the apples are tender. Remove from the oven and leave to cool in the tin.

LAVENHAM GUILDHALL

Lavenham is an almost unspoilt medieval town with streets of crooked half-timbered houses and a glorious late fifteenth-century church financed with profits from the wool trade. Apart from the church, one of the best buildings is the guildhall, prominently sited in the market square. Traditionally timber-framed, the upper floor is jettied out over the lower and both are lit with oriel windows. The building is supported on a substantial brick and rubble plinth, very evident where the ground slopes away towards Lady Street.

The hall was built in about 1528-9 by the Guild of Corpus Christi, one of three in the town founded to regulate the wool trade. The guild was dissolved only thirty or so years later, since when the hall has served as townhall, prison, workhouse, almshouse and wool store. Today, as well as housing a small museum, it is used for public meetings and local social activities.

Paradise Slice

Makes 10 slices

6oz (175g) shortcrust pastry
  (see page 16)
4oz (100g) margarine, softened
4oz (100g) caster sugar
1 egg, beaten

2oz (50g) semolina
2oz (50g) shredded coconut
2oz (50g) glacé cherries, chopped
2oz (50g) walnuts, chopped
6oz (175g) sultanas

Make the pastry according to the instructions on page 16 and chill for at least 15 minutes. Preheat the oven to gas mark 5/375°F/190°C. Grease a 7 × 11in (17·5 × 27·5cm) Swiss roll tin. On a lightly floured board, roll out the pastry and use to line the prepared tin. Beat together the margarine and sugar until light and fluffy. Add the egg and beat again. Add the remaining ingredients and mix thoroughly. Turn into the pastry case and smooth. Bake for 20–25 minutes until golden and firm. Remove from the oven and leave to cool in the tin. When cold, cut into pieces and lift carefully from the tin.

Oh some are fond of Spanish wine, and some are fond of French,
And some'll swallow tay and stuff fit only for a wench.

John Masefield (1878-1967), 'Captain Stratton's Fancy'

Suffolk Rusks

Makes 16-18 rusks

FOR THE RUSKS

8oz (225g) self-raising flour, sifted
4oz (100g) margarine, softened

1 egg, beaten
a pinch of salt

FOR THE TOPPING

4oz (100g) mature Cheddar cheese,
  finely grated

a little cream or top of the milk
a pinch of cayenne pepper

Preheat the oven to gas mark 7/425°F/220°C. Grease a baking tray. Rub the fat into the flour until the mixture resembles breadcrumbs, then add the beaten egg and the salt and mix to a soft dough. On a lightly floured board, roll out to a thickness of about ¼in (0·5cm). Cut into rounds using a 2½in (6cm) cutter and place on the prepared tray. Bake for 15 minutes until golden brown, then remove from the oven, tear or cut in half and put back into the oven. Bake for a further 15-20 minutes until dried out. Meanwhile mix together the ingredients for the topping. Remove the rusks from the oven and spread with the cheese topping. Place under a hot grill for a few minutes to melt the topping and then serve hot.

These are a traditional East Anglian speciality, served with butter and jam, or with a cheese topping as in the tea-room at Lavenham.

WIMPOLE HALL

When Rudyard Kipling visited his daughter Elsie here, a few months after she and her husband Captain George Bambridge took up residence in 1936, he was moved to remark that he hoped she had not bitten off more than she could chew. Two years later the Bambridges embarked on the restoration and refurnishing of the largest house in Cambridgeshire, whose red-brick and stone façades, three and four storeys high in the central block, stretch nearly 300 feet from end to end.

The largely eighteenth-century façades added to the original seventeenth-century core date from Wimpole's golden age. From 1713-40 the house belonged to Edward Harley, 2nd Earl of Oxford, who entertained Swift and Pope among a brilliant circle of writers, scholars and artists. James Gibbs's baroque chapel and long library are principal features, but Wimpole's crowning glory is John Soane's Yellow Drawing Room, added by the 3rd Earl of Hardwicke.

A letter from Twinings to Mrs Bambridge in May 1950 reveals that, during the years of rationing after the Second World War, Wimpole's tea coupons were entrusted to the firm in exchange for regular supplies of tea. Correspondence over the next three years shows that the family continued to order Indian tea from Twinings, usually in fourteen-pound cases at 4s a pound but sometimes in five-pound packets. The array of tea caddies dotted around the house would, when in use, have been filled from huge metal chests in the housekeeper's dry store in the basement. These are on casters so that they could be wheeled in and out of their storage space, and they were kept padlocked, along with containers of coffee, cocoa, barley and other household ingredients, because of the risk of pilfering by the servants.

Date and Oat Slices

Makes 15 squares

8oz (225g) dates, roughly chopped
3oz (75g) shredded coconut
3oz (75g) porridge oats
3oz (75g) plain wholemeal flour, sifted

1½ oz (40g) light soft brown sugar
¾ teaspoon baking powder
6oz (175g) margarine, softened
demerara sugar for sprinkling

Preheat the oven to gas mark 4/350°F/180°C. Grease an 11 × 7in (27·5 × 17·5cm) Swiss roll tin. Cover the dates with water and simmer until soft. Mix together the dry ingredients and rub in the margarine to form a crumbly mixture. Sprinkle half the mixture into the prepared tin and press down lightly. Spread the softened dates over the base and add the remaining crumbly mixture. Spread evenly, press down lightly and sprinkle liberally with demerara sugar. Bake for 25–30 minutes until browned. Remove from the oven, leave to cool in the tin and then cut into squares.

Ginger and Treacle Scones

Makes 11 scones

8oz (225g) self-raising flour, sifted
1½ teaspoons baking powder
2 teaspoons ground ginger
2oz (50g) margarine, softened and cut into small pieces

6 tablespoons milk
1 rounded tablespoon black treacle
a little milk to glaze

Preheat the oven to gas mark 7/425°F/220°C. Grease a baking tray. Mix together the flour, baking powder and ginger and rub in the fat until the mixture resembles breadcrumbs. Warm the milk and treacle together in a small pan until lukewarm. Add to the mixture and mix with a round-bladed knife to a soft dough. On a lightly floured board, knead until smooth then roll out to a thickness of ¾in (1·5cm). Cut into rounds using a 2in (5cm) cutter and place on the prepared tray. Brush the tops with a little milk. Bake just above the centre of the oven for 10–15 minutes until well risen and golden brown. Remove from the oven and lift on to a wire rack to cool. Serve warm or cold with butter.

Regional Specialities

Grantham Gingerbreads

Makes approximately 30 biscuits

4oz (100g) butter or margarine, softened
12oz (350g) caster sugar

1 egg, beaten
9oz (250g) self-raising flour, sifted
1 teaspoon ground ginger

Preheat the oven to gas mark 2/300°F/150°C. Grease two or three baking trays. Beat together the fat and sugar until light and fluffy. Add the egg and beat well. Add the flour and ginger and mix to a firm dough. Form into balls about the size of a walnut and place on the prepared tray, leaving room for the biscuits to spread. Bake for 40-45 minutes until crisp, hollow and light brown. Remove from the oven and leave on the trays for a few minutes before lifting on to a wire rack to cool.

These biscuits were originally baked as fairings for the Grantham Fair. Cakes and biscuits for fairs and revels were usually made in large quantities and then given away or sold cheaply. During the eighteenth century spices and dried fruit gradually became more readily available and were used instead of sugar to sweeten and give flavour to cakes.

Norfolk Tart

Makes 1 × 7in (17·5cm) round tart

6oz (175g) rich shortcrust pastry (see page 16)
4oz (100g) golden syrup
½oz (15g) butter

the grated rind of half a lemon
2 tablespoons double cream
1 egg

Make the pastry according to the instructions on page 16 and chill for at least 15 minutes. Preheat the oven to gas mark 6/400°F/200°C. Grease a 7in (17·5cm) round flan tin or dish. On a floured board, roll out the pastry to make a circle and use to line the prepared tin or dish. Bake blind for 15-20 minutes. Remove from the oven and lift out the baking beans and paper. Reduce the oven temperature to gas mark 4/350°F/180°C. Warm the syrup with the butter and lemon rind until the butter has dissolved. Beat the cream and egg together and add to the mixture. Pour into the pastry case and bake for 20 minutes until golden and firm. Remove from the oven and serve warm or cold.

This delicious traditional tart is ideal served at tea-time or as a dessert with whipped or clotted cream.

A Yorkshire Tea, clockwise from left: Old Peculier fruit cake (page 102); Scarborough muffins (page 108); fat rascals (page 107); Yorkshire curd cheesecake (page 99).

Suffolk Apple Cake

Makes 1 × 8in (20cm) round cake

8oz (225g) plain flour, sifted
1½ teaspoons baking powder
a pinch of salt
4oz (100g) lard or dripping

8oz (225g) eating apples (weighed after being peeled and cored), finely chopped or grated
1½ tablespoons caster, granulated or demerara sugar
1–2 tablespoons milk

Preheat the oven to gas mark 4/350°F/180°C. Grease a baking tray. Mix together the flour, baking powder and salt and rub in the fat. Add the apples, sugar and enough milk to give a soft dough. Place the dough on the prepared tray and shape with the hands into a flat round cake approximately 8in (20cm) across and ½–¾in (1–1·5cm) thick. Bake for 40–45 minutes until golden and firm. Remove from the oven and serve hot, split and buttered.

Suffolk Cakes

Makes 10 buns

2 eggs, separated
4oz (100g) caster sugar
the grated rind of half a lemon

2oz (50g) butter, softened
2oz (50g) plain flour, sifted

Preheat the oven to gas mark 6/400°F/200°C. Place paper cases in ten patty tins. Beat the egg whites until very stiff. Beat the egg yolks and add to the whites with the sugar, lemon rind and butter. Beat well. Fold in the flour and spoon the mixture into the paper cases. Bake for 10–15 minutes until pale golden and firm. Remove from the oven and lift carefully on to a wire rack to cool.

An Irish Tea, clockwise from left: barm brack (page 140); boiled whiskey cake (page 133), Irish potato cakes (page 142).

Suffolk Fourses

Makes approximately
16 cakes

1oz (25g) fresh yeast
1 teaspoon caster sugar
10fl oz (300ml) milk
2lb (900g) plain flour, sifted
½ teaspoon salt
2oz (50g) lard, softened
4oz (100g) caster, granulated or
    demerara sugar

4oz (100g) currants or raisins
a pinch of mixed spice
6oz (175g) butter
3 eggs, well beaten
caster or demerara sugar for
    dredging

Cream the yeast with the teaspoon of caster sugar. Warm the milk and add to the yeast. Mix together the flour and salt and rub in the fat. Add the sugar, currants or raisins and spice and mix well. Melt the butter and stir into the beaten eggs. Add to the milk and yeast mixture and pour into the flour. Mix with a round-bladed knife to a light dough. Cover the bowl with a clean damp cloth and leave in a warm place for about 2 hours until the dough has doubled in size. Meanwhile grease two baking trays. When the dough has risen knead on a lightly floured board, then roll out to a thickness of approximately ¾in (1·5cm) and cut into rounds 4in (10cm) in diameter. Place on the prepared trays and leave to rise in a warm place for 30 minutes. Meanwhile heat the oven to gas mark 6/400°F/200°C. When the fourses have risen, mark the tops into four sections and dredge with caster or demerara sugar. Bake for 15-20 minutes until firm and golden. Remove from the oven and eat warm or cold, split and buttered.

Heart of England

Gingerbreads have always been popular in the Midlands, and until the early 1900s Birmingham held two gingerbread fairs every year, one at Whitsuntide (seven weeks after Easter) and one at Michaelmas (29 September), as stipulated by Royal Charter. All sorts of different gingerbreads were sold on the market stalls around St Martin's Church. The earliest were solid slabs made with flour, honey and ginger. The mixture was usually pressed into moulds, then baked and gilded, or it was cut into biscuit-like rounds. Sponge gingerbreads as we know them today started to appear in recipe books in the mid-nineteenth century when raising agents began to be more widely available.

The best-known cakes from the Midlands are Bakewell tarts from Derbyshire and Banbury cakes from Oxfordshire. The description Bakewell 'tarts' is frowned upon in the town itself, where the original – and more exciting – Bakewell pudding has been baked to a secret recipe for hundreds of years. Banbury cakes are thought to date back to pagan days and have always had strong connections with May Day celebrations. Recipes have changed greatly over the centuries, varying from a type of fruited bread flavoured with caraway seeds, to pastry cases filled with fruit, saffron and sherry, to the fruit-filled pastry crust that we know today. The recipe is similar to that for Lancashire's Eccles cakes, the difference being that Banbury cakes are generally smaller and oval, whereas Eccles cakes are round. The pastry should be very brittle and the cakes should be eaten hot.

Cecil Porter of Gemini News Service once wrote:
'Tea is much more than a mere drink in Britain. It is a solace, a mystique, an art, a way of life, almost a religion. It is more deeply traditional than the roast beef of old England . . . This khaki-coloured concoction, brewed through an accident of history from an exotic plant grown thousands of miles from fog, cricket and left-handed driving, has become the life-blood of the nation.'

CALKE ABBEY

Calke Abbey lies buried in its beautiful eighteenth-century park, hidden from the world. It was built in 1701–4, but the grey sandstone façades and the balustraded roofline conceal the substantial remains of earlier buildings, some of the stonework perhaps recycled from the priory of Austin canons established here in the early twelfth century.

Calke has been in the hands of the same family for hundreds of years, each generation of the Harpurs and Harpur Crewes contributing to the extraordinary individuality of the house. The collection of stuffed birds and geological specimens in the salon reflects the interests of Sir Vauncey Harpur Crewe, the idiosyncratic recluse who inherited Calke in 1886. Increasingly unpredictable, Sir Vauncey took to communicating with his servants by letter, would make off to the woods when his wife entertained, and forbade his tenants to cut hedges so as to provide maximum cover for the birds.

The Chinese silk hangings for the sumptuous state bed were found in a packing case, and many more gems lay forgotten behind closed doors or languishing in outhouses – Victorian dolls in mint condition, a Georgian chamber organ and a harpsichord by Burckhardt Shudi. Household objects which would have been thrown away long ago in other establishments have also survived here.

Melbourne Wakes Cakes

Makes approximately 24 cakes

14oz (400g) plain flour, sifted
8oz (225g) butter, softened
4oz (100g) caster sugar
2oz (50g) currants

1 egg, beaten
1 tablespoon double cream
caster sugar for dredging

Preheat the oven to gas mark 4/350°F/180°C. Grease two or three baking trays. Rub the butter into the flour and add the sugar and currants. Add the egg and cream and mix to a soft dough. On a lightly floured board, roll out to a thickness of ¼in (0·5cm) and cut into rounds using a 3in (7·5cm) cutter. Place on the prepared trays and bake for 10–15 minutes until lightly browned. Remove from the oven and dredge immediately with caster sugar. Leave to cool on the trays for 5 minutes before lifting on to a wire rack to cool completely.

These Derbyshire biscuits were traditionally made for the annual revel or wake which celebrated the anniversary of each church's patron saint. Very often the celebrations stretched over two days: the Sunday for church services and the Monday for village sports and festivities.

Moorland Tarts

Makes 12 tarts

8oz (225g) shortcrust pastry
 (see page 16)
2 hard-boiled eggs, chopped
4oz (100g) mixed candied peel

4oz (100g) currants
½ teaspoon grated nutmeg
3oz (75g) margarine, softened
4oz (100g) caster sugar

Make the pastry according to the instructions on page 16 and chill for at least 15 minutes. Preheat the oven to gas mark 7/425°F/220°C. Grease twelve patty tins. On a floured board, roll out the pastry and cut out circles using a 3in (7·5cm) cutter. Use to line the patty tins. Combine all the remaining ingredients and put 1 teaspoon of the mixture into each pastry case. Bake for 10-15 minutes until the pastry is golden. Remove from the oven and leave to cool in the tins for 10-15 minutes before lifting carefully on to a wire rack to cool completely.

This is a traditional Derbyshire recipe. Although the filling of hard-boiled eggs, dried fruit and sugar sounds strange, the tarts are really tasty.

CANONS ASHBY

Set in the rolling, thinly populated country of south Northamptonshire, this ancient courtyard house seems lost in a time warp. John Dryden's modest H-shaped Tudor manor, built with material from the demolished east end of the priory church which gave Canons Ashby its name, now forms the great-hall range of the house. Later additions were made by his son Sir Erasmus, and in 1708-10 Edward Dryden remodelled the south front. He made his money from the grocery trade, and tea obviously played an important part in his life: a silver tea kettle made specially for him and now on display in the dining-room bears witness to this.

Tea parties were a common occurrence at Canons Ashby, and an amusing story tells how Sir Henry Dryden, the much-loved Victorian squire known as the Antiquary, decided one day to invite a few friends to afternoon tea on the lawn. Before the party began the local postman had delivered the mail, and, as he was also the man who clipped the hedges, Sir Henry asked if he would trim the yew trees. As they sipped their tea and watched the postman clipping away, the guests decided to prevail upon this talented man by asking him to give them all a haircut. (It is not known whether his clippers served a dual purpose or whether perhaps he carried with him all the tools he might be called upon to use in one day!) He eventually joined the tea party, having completed the various tasks set him. From then on people would try to secure an invitation to tea on the lawn with Sir Henry in order also to get a free haircut.

Canons Ashby Coconut Cake

Makes 12 fingers

FOR THE CAKE
4oz (100g) margarine, softened
3oz (75g) light soft brown sugar
2 teaspoons almond essence
the grated rind of 1 lemon

1 egg, beaten
9oz (250g) plain flour, sifted
5–6 tablespoons plum jam

FOR THE TOPPING
1 egg, beaten
3oz (75g) light soft brown sugar

4oz (100g) shredded coconut

FOR DIPPING
6–8oz (175–225g) milk or plain
*   chocolate*

Preheat the oven to gas mark 4/350°F/180°C. Grease a 7 × 11in (17·5 × 27·5cm) Swiss roll tin. Beat together the margarine, sugar, almond essence, lemon rind and egg. Add the flour and mix well. Press into the prepared tin and spread a layer of jam on top. Mix together the ingredients for the topping and spread over the jam. Bake for 20–30 minutes until firm and pale golden. Remove from the oven and leave to cool in the tin. When cold, cut into fingers and lift carefully from the tin. Melt the chocolate and dip both ends of each finger into it. Place carefully on a wire rack to set.

Toffee Bars

Makes 12 bars

FOR THE CAKE
4oz (100g) butter, softened
4oz (100g) light soft brown sugar
1 egg yolk

2oz (50g) plain flour, sifted
2oz (50g) porridge oats

FOR THE TOPPING
3oz (75g) plain chocolate
1oz (25g) butter

2oz (50g) walnuts or almonds,
*   chopped*

Preheat the oven to gas mark 5/375°F/190°C. Grease a 7 × 11in (17·5 × 27·5cm) Swiss roll tin. Beat together the butter, sugar and egg yolk until light and smooth. Add the flour and oats and mix well. Press into the prepared tin and bake for 15-20 minutes until lightly browned. Remove from the oven and leave to cool slightly in the tin. Melt together the chocolate and butter for the topping and spread over the cake. Cover with the chopped nuts and leave to set. While still warm, cut into bars and leave in the tin until completely cold.

CLIVEDEN

This three-storey Italianate palace high above the River Thames is the masterpiece of Sir Charles Barry, built in 1850-1 for the Duke and Duchess of Sutherland. An inscription running below the roofline parapet records the earlier building here which was destroyed by fire – a Restoration house by William Winde for the 2nd Duke of Buckingham, much of whose character Barry preserved – as well as the construction of the present mansion.

The Duke of Sutherland's wife was an intimate friend of Queen Victoria, and the Queen often travelled by boat from Windsor to take tea with the Duchess on the banks of the river. In the grounds of the house there is a small octagonal temple which served as a tea house and was another favourite spot for afternoon tea. The temple gives spectacular views over the river and the surrounding countryside, and the idea was to enjoy the view and then to retire to the grotto under the temple for tea. The grotto, like other tea houses and summer pavilions, contained tea-making equipment so that tea parties and picnics could be enjoyed with the minimum amount of fuss. On large estates a whole day was set aside for such outings; the assembly made their way on foot or by horse and carriage to the appointed rendezvous, indulged in a leisurely lunch or tea and then returned in the late afternoon.

The garden as it is today owes much to the 1st Viscount Astor, who bought the house in 1893. Amongst other things, he laid out the Italianate long garden and the informal water garden. The 2nd Viscount Astor and his wife Nancy made Cliveden famous as a centre of literary and political society, entertaining, among others, Henry James, who wrote: 'There are few hours in life more agreeable than the hour dedicated to the ceremony known as afternoon tea.'

If you are cold, tea will warm you;
if you are heated, it will cool you;
if you are depressed, it will cheer you;
if you are exhausted, it will calm you.

William Gladstone (1809-98)

Carob Crunch

Makes 12 pieces

8oz (225g) margarine
1oz (25g) carob powder
8oz (225g) plain wholemeal flour, sifted

5oz (150g) light or dark soft brown sugar
4oz (100g) shredded coconut

Preheat the oven to gas mark 5/375°F/190°C. Grease a 7 × 11in (17·5 × 27·5cm) Swiss roll tin. In a medium-sized pan, melt the margarine and add the carob powder. Stir over a gentle heat until the carob is dissolved. Add the flour, sugar and coconut and mix well. Turn into the prepared tin and press well down. Smooth the top and bake for 20-25 minutes until firm. Remove from the oven and leave to cool in the tin. When cold, cut into pieces and lift from the tin.

This is an excellent recipe for anybody who cannot eat chocolate. Carob powder is generally available in health-food shops.

Herb Bread

Makes 1 × 1lb (450g) loaf

8oz (225g) self-raising white or wholemeal flour (or a mixture of half and half), sifted
1 teaspoon dry English mustard powder
2 teaspoons fresh chopped herbs (chives, thyme, basil, sage, parsley), or more to taste

4oz (100g) mature Cheddar cheese, grated
1oz (25g) margarine
1 egg, beaten
5fl oz (150ml) water

Preheat the oven to gas mark 5/375°F/190°C. Grease a 1lb (450g) loaf tin. Mix together the flour, mustard powder, herbs and cheese. Melt the margarine, add to the mixture with the egg and water and mix to a soft, wet, cake-like dough. Turn into the prepared tin and bake for 45 minutes until well risen and golden brown. Remove from the oven and turn out on to a wire rack to cool. Serve warm or cold with butter.

Pour, varlet, pour the water,
The water steaming hot!
A spoonful for each man of us,
Another for the pot!

Thomas Babington Macaulay (1800-59)

HIDCOTE MANOR GARDEN

The mother of Lawrence Johnston bought her only surviving son this property at the northern end of the Cotswolds, with its pleasant seventeenth-century manor house, 280 acres of farmland and a lovely view west over the Vale of Evesham. There was no garden. The bones of what is now one of Europe's most famous layouts emerged over seven years of relentlessly hard work from 1905.

The garden is only ten acres in all, but the numerous outdoor rooms into which it is divided make it seem much larger. Each hedged compartment has its own character, and everywhere there are rare and unusual plants from all over the world, some of them the fruits of Lawrence Johnston's expeditions to South Africa in 1927 and to China in 1931. There are several examples of the varieties he raised and selected, such as Hidcote hypericum and the deep-yellow rose 'Lawrence Johnston'.

Legend has it that the National Trust's first catering enterprise consisted of a cup of tea and a bun served through the window of a gardener's cottage at Hidcote, perhaps reflecting the same spirit of enterprise which Lawrence Johnston had exhibited in creating his world-famous garden from scratch.

American Zucchini Cake

Makes 1 × 2lb (900g) loaf

2 eggs
4fl oz (100ml) oil (corn, vegetable, sunflower or safflower)
8oz (225g) caster sugar
12oz (350g) grated courgettes
1½ teaspoons vanilla or almond essence

2oz (50g) chopped nuts or a mixture of 1oz (25g) chopped nuts and 1oz (25g) sultanas
6oz (175g) self-raising flour, sifted
1½ teaspoons ground cinnamon or mixed spice

Preheat the oven to gas mark 3/325°F/160°C. Grease and line a 2lb (900g) loaf tin. Beat the eggs until light and foamy. Add the oil, sugar, courgettes and essence and mix lightly, until all the ingredients are evenly distributed. Fold in the nuts (or nuts and sultanas), flour and spice until well mixed and turn into the prepared tin. Bake for 1¼-1½ hours until a skewer comes out clean. Remove from the oven and turn out on to a wire rack to cool.

This is an excellent, unusual, moist cake.

Dolce Torinese

Makes 1 × 8in (20cm)
round cake

4oz (100g) good-quality plain
 chocolate
1½ tablespoons sherry, brandy
 or rum
4oz (100g) unsalted butter, softened
5oz (150g) caster sugar
1 egg, separated

2½ oz (65g) blanched almonds,
 shredded
6 butter biscuits, broken into small
 pieces
icing sugar for dredging
whipped cream (optional)

Grease and line an 8in (20cm) round, loose-bottomed tin. Melt the
chocolate and stir in the alcohol. Beat the butter, sugar and egg yolk until
light and fluffy. Stir in the almonds and the chocolate mixture. Beat the
egg white until very stiff and fold into the mixture. Add the broken
biscuits and stir until evenly distributed. Turn into the prepared tin and
smooth the top. Place the tin in the refrigerator and leave to set
overnight. When ready to serve, turn out and dust with icing sugar. If
liked, pipe whipped cream around the edge, or serve separately.

This rich cake makes an excellent dessert for a special dinner party.

KEDLESTON HALL

Kedleston was always intended as a showpiece. Sir Nathaniel Curzon,
later 1st Lord Scarsdale, began the house in 1759, only a year after he
had inherited the estate. A cultivated man who was interested in the arts,
he saw it as a setting for his collection of paintings and sculpture – on
view to visitors from the day the house was built. The formal reception
rooms and guest suite filling the three-storey central block were never
intended to be used except for the entertainment of important guests.
The family lived in one of the rectangular pavilions on either side, with
the kitchen and domestic offices in the other.

Although work began under the direction of Matthew Brettingham
and James Paine, by 1760 these two architects had been superseded by
the young Robert Adam, recently returned from Rome. Notes from
1766 give a hint as to the current fashion in furniture. Apparently Sir
Nathaniel had considered having marble console tables under the pier-
glass in the music-room, but Adam instructed him that 'marble tables
are not so proper for a withdrawing room as card tables or tables for tea
china'. In the seventeenth and eighteenth centuries tea-making was
considered to be too much of an art to leave to the servants; when giving
a tea party, it was the lady of the house who brewed the tea. She would
have all the necessary equipment arranged on a low table near her chair,
and smaller tables were placed beside guests' armchairs for their cups and

saucers. Until the late nineteenth century, side plates were not normally part of the tea service, as any food handed round was so delicate that it could be placed on the saucer or eaten immediately with the fingers.

Cherry Bakewells

Makes 20 tarts

8oz (225g) shortcrust pastry
    (see page 16)
2oz (50g) strawberry jam
4oz (100g) butter or margarine,
    softened
4oz (100g) caster sugar
2 eggs

2oz (50g) ground almonds
2oz (50g) self-raising flour, sifted
1 teaspoon almond essence
6oz (175g) icing sugar, sifted
1–2 tablespoons water
20 cherries (fresh, stoned or glacé)

Make the pastry according to the instructions on page 16 and chill for at least 15 minutes. Preheat the oven to gas mark 6/400°F/200°C. Grease twenty patty tins. On a lightly floured board, roll out the pastry and cut twenty circles using a 3in (7·5cm) cutter. Use to line the prepared tins and spread a little jam in the base of each. Beat together the fat and caster sugar, then beat in the eggs, one at a time, adding half the ground almonds after each one. Add the flour and almond essence and stir well. Spoon the mixture into the pastry cases and bake for 20 minutes until well risen, firm and golden. Remove from the oven and leave to cool in the tins. Mix together the icing sugar and water and, when the tarts are cold, spoon the icing on to the top. Decorate each with a cherry.

Kedleston Marmalade Cake

Makes 1 × 8in (20cm) round cake

6oz (175g) margarine, softened
2oz (50g) light or dark soft brown
    sugar
4 tablespoons golden syrup
2 eggs
5oz (150g) orange marmalade

10oz (275g) self-raising wholemeal
    flour, sifted
2 teaspoons baking powder
½ teaspoon ground ginger
3–4 tablespoons orange juice

Preheat the oven to gas mark 4/350°F/180°C. Grease and line an 8in (20cm) round tin. Beat together the margarine and sugar until light and fluffy. Add the syrup and beat again. Whisk together the eggs and marmalade and add to the mixture with the flour, baking powder and ginger. Stir in the orange juice to give a soft, dropping consistency. Turn into the prepared tin and bake for about 1 hour until a skewer comes out clean. Remove from the oven and leave to cool in the tin for 15 minutes before turning out on to a wire rack to cool completely.

LONGSHAW ESTATE

It is difficult to believe that the 1,700 acres of the Longshaw Estate are only ten miles south-west of the centre of Sheffield. Although it lies on millstone grit, the estate is altogether much softer in character and more varied than the great open moors of the High Peak. Burbage Brook, which runs through the area, provides interest all year round, as it can change from a gently flowing stream in summer to a gushing cascade in the wet season. The great abandoned quarries at Bolehill are a reminder of the estate's importance as a major centre of quarrying in the nine-teenth century. For centuries Bolehill was the source of millstones for the local water-powered mills, and stone was taken from here for the Derwent and Howden dams. Numerous worked or half-worked stones still remain.

To the east, in an attractive landscape of mixed woodland, heather and coppice, stands Longshaw Lodge. Built in the 1820s as a shooting box for the Duke of Rutland, it now houses the Trust's tea-room.

Cheese and Celery Whirls

Makes approximately 10 whirls

12oz (350g) self-raising flour, sifted
1 teaspoon salt
½ teaspoon dry English mustard powder
2oz (50g) margarine, softened
4oz (100g) mature Cheddar cheese, grated

1 garlic clove (or more to taste), crushed
1 egg, beaten
5fl oz (150ml) milk
3-4 sticks of celery, washed and roughly chopped

Preheat the oven to gas mark 7/425°F/220°C. Mix together the flour, salt and mustard powder. Rub in the margarine until the mixture resembles breadcrumbs. Add most of the grated cheese (reserving a little for sprinkling on top), garlic, beaten egg and milk and mix well so that all the ingredients are evenly distributed. On a floured board, knead lightly and then roll out to a rectangle approximately 9 × 12in (22·5 × 30cm). Scatter the celery over the surface. Roll up like a Swiss roll, starting with the narrow edge. Cut slices approximately ¼in (1·5cm) thick, lay them flat on the prepared trays and sprinkle a little of the remaining cheese over the surface of each. Bake for 15–20 minutes until golden and well risen. Remove from the oven and serve warm.

These pretty whirls make an excellent accompaniment to a dinner-party starter or they are suitable served as a tea-time savoury. They are beautifully light and extremely tasty.

Longshaw Tart

Makes 20 slices

12oz (350g) shortcrust pastry
(see page 16)
6-7 tablespoons jam (raspberry,
strawberry or apricot)
9oz (250g) margarine, softened
9oz (250g) granulated sugar

4½ oz (115g) peanuts, finely
chopped
4½ oz (115g) fresh breadcrumbs
(white or wholemeal)
3 eggs, beaten
1½ teaspoons almond essence

Make the pastry according to the instructions on page 16 and chill for at least 15 minutes. Preheat the oven to gas mark 5/375°F/190°C. Grease a 10 × 12 × 1½in (25 × 30 × 3·5cm) tin. On a floured board, roll out the pastry to make a rectangle to fit the tin and use to line the base. Spread the jam over the pastry. Beat together the margarine and sugar until light and fluffy. Add the peanuts, breadcrumbs, beaten eggs and almond essence and mix well. Turn into the pastry case and bake for 25-30 minutes until firm and golden. Remove from the oven and leave to cool in the tin. When cold, cut into slices and lift carefully out of the tin.

Regional Specialities

Banbury Cakes

Makes 11-12 cakes

12oz (350g) puff pastry
(see page 15)
2oz (50g) butter
4oz (100g) currants
2oz (50g) mixed candied peel
¼ teaspoon ground cinnamon
½ teaspoon allspice or grated nutmeg

1oz (25g) light or dark soft brown
sugar
1 tablespoon dark rum
a little milk or water
1 egg white, lightly beaten
caster sugar for dredging

Make the pastry according to the instructions on page 15 and chill for at least 30 minutes. Melt the butter in a small pan and add the dried fruit, spices, brown sugar and rum. Stir and leave to cool. Preheat the oven to gas mark 8/450°F/230°C. Grease two baking trays. On a lightly floured board, roll out the pastry to a thickness of ¼in (0·5cm) and cut into rounds approximately 4in (10cm) in diameter. Place a spoonful of the fruit mixture on each circle, dampen the edges of the pastry with a little milk or water and gather the edges together. Seal well, turn each cake over and roll gently to a neat oval shape. Cut three slashes in the top and place on prepared trays. Brush the tops with the beaten egg white and dredge with caster sugar. Bake for 10-15 minutes until golden. Remove from oven and lift on to a wire rack to cool slightly before serving.

Derbyshire Spiced Easter Fruit Bread

Makes 1 × 2lb (900g) loaf

8oz (225g) self-raising flour, sifted
1 teaspoon mixed spice
½ teaspoon ground cinnamon
3oz (75g) lard, softened
3oz (75g) sugar

2oz (50g) sultanas
2oz (50g) dates, chopped
1 egg, beaten
6 tablespoons milk

Preheat the oven to gas mark 5/375°F/190°C. Grease and line a 2lb (900g) loaf tin. Mix together the flour and spices. Chop the lard into very small pieces and cut roughly into the flour with a knife. Add the sugar, sultanas, dates, egg and milk and mix to a soft consistency. Turn into the prepared tin and bake for 40–45 minutes until a skewer comes out clean. Remove from the oven and turn out on to a wire rack to cool. Serve sliced with butter.

Gloucester Apple Shortbread

Makes 1×7in (17.5cm) round cake

1lb (450g) cooking apples
2-3 tablespoons light soft brown or
   demerara sugar (or to taste)
4oz (100g) butter, softened

3oz (75g) caster sugar
1 egg, beaten
6oz (175g) plain flour, sifted

Peel, core and chop the apples. Stew gently with the brown sugar until soft. Remove from the heat and leave to cool. Preheat the oven to gas mark 4/350°F/180°C. Grease a 7in (17·5cm) round sandwich tin. Beat together the butter and caster sugar until light and creamy. Add the egg and flour and work to a soft dough. Divide into two portions. On a lightly floured board, roll out one portion to make a circle to fit the prepared tin. Place in the tin and spoon the apples on top. Roll out the second portion of dough and use to cover the apples. Mark the top into eight segments and prick lightly all over with a fork. Bake for 1 hour until crisp and golden. Remove from oven and leave to cool in the tin.

The North-East

As in the lowlands of Scotland, oats have always been widely grown in Northumberland and Yorkshire; oatcakes and oatmeal breads and parkins are therefore very much part of the regional diet. Gingerbreads too, closely associated with Hallowe'en and Guy Fawkes's Night, are a favourite. Open tarts and curd cheesecakes are served as puddings or cakes, and in the past provided an opportunity to use up some of the plentiful eggs and curd cheese available after the Lent fast.

Several of the regional specialities have acquired unusual names over the years. Fat Rascals from Yorkshire are fruity biscuits; Singin' Hinny is a larded dough that hisses or sings as it cooks, a noise that is caused by the large amount of fat in the dough; Stottie cake is a flat bread that makes delicious sandwiches and a good accompaniment to cheese; and Sly cake is a pastry case filled with all sorts of dried fruit.

One of Yorkshire's best-known pastries is Wilfra Apple Cake, made with the local Wensleydale cheese. It was traditionally baked in Ripon on St Wilfrid's Day (the first or second Saturday of August) to celebrate the return of the saint to his home town after a long absence abroad. A second speciality for the festival were little almond cheesecakes, Wilfra tarts, which the residents of the town would make by the dozen and place outside their front doors so that passers-by could help themselves.

BENINGBROUGH HALL

Finished in 1716, Beningbrough Hall is a product of the cultivated, secure decades of the early eighteenth century. Built for John Bourchier, whose family had acquired the property by marriage in the previous century, the construction was supervised by the local carpenter-architect William Thornton, who was also responsible for the woodcarvings which are such a feature of the house.

The formality of early eighteenth-century life is reflected in the suite of state rooms for honoured guests traditionally sited on the ground floor, and in the long saloon used for balls and large family gatherings. Another insight is provided by the intimate closets where important guests could receive their closest friends or relax in private, drinking tea, reading or writing. Always richly decorated, the closets at Beningbrough are crowded with Oriental porcelain displayed on stepped ledges over the fireplaces. The idea was made fashionable by Queen Mary II when she came back from Holland, and the showing off of fine china was considered to be a demonstration of wealth and good taste.

As Beningbrough was built before dining-rooms had evolved as special features, the house is displayed as it would have appeared at the time. If John Bourchier wanted tea, or indeed other refreshments, he would simply have asked a servant to fetch a table, and whatever else was needed, and place it wherever it was required.

Madeira Cake

Makes 1 × 7in (17·5cm) round cake

8oz (225g) plain flour, sifted
1 teaspoon baking powder
6oz (175g) butter or margarine, softened

6oz (175g) caster sugar
the grated rind of half a lemon
3 eggs
2 tablespoons milk

Preheat the oven to gas mark 4/350°F/180°C. Grease and line a 7in (17·5cm) round tin. Mix together the flour and baking powder. Beat together the butter or margarine, sugar and lemon rind until light and fluffy. Beat in the eggs, one at a time, adding 2 tablespoons of flour with the last two. Fold in the remaining flour, then gently mix in the milk. Turn into the prepared tin and bake for 1 hour until a skewer comes out clean. Remove from the oven and turn out on to a wire rack to cool.

Marmalade Cake

Makes 1 × 7in (17·5cm) round cake

8oz (225g) self-raising flour, sifted
1 teaspoon mixed spice
6oz (175g) butter or margarine, softened
6oz (175g) light soft brown sugar
3 eggs

2 tablespoons thick orange marmalade
3oz (75g) mixed dried fruit
the grated rind and juice of 1 orange
2 tablespoons milk

Preheat the oven to gas mark 4/350°F/180°C. Grease and line a 7in (17·5cm) round tin. Mix together the flour and spice. Beat together the butter or margarine and sugar until light and fluffy. Beat in the eggs, one at a time, adding 2 tablespoons of flour with the last two. Fold in the remaining flour, marmalade, mixed dried fruit, orange juice and rind. Add the milk and distribute the ingredients evenly. Turn into the prepared tin and bake for 1½ hours until a skewer comes out clean. Remove from the oven and turn out on to a wire rack to cool.

Treacle Tart

Makes 12 portions

FOR THE PASTRY
8oz (225g) plain flour, sifted
2oz (50g) lard or other shortening,
  softened

2oz (50g) margarine, softened
1oz (25g) caster sugar
a little cold water

FOR THE FILLING
1lb (450g) golden syrup
4–6oz (100–175g) fresh white
  breadcrumbs

the juice of half a lemon

Make the pastry by rubbing the fats into the flour. Add the sugar and enough water to mix to a soft but pliable dough. Knead lightly, wrap in foil or cling film and chill for at least 15 minutes. Preheat the oven to gas mark 4/350°F/180°C. Grease a 12in (30cm) round flan dish. On a floured board, roll out the pastry to fit the prepared dish and use to line the base and sides. Place the syrup in a pan and warm gently. Remove from the heat, add the breadcrumbs and lemon juice and leave until the bread is well soaked. If the mixture is dry, add a little more syrup. Turn the mixture into the pastry case and spread evenly. Bake for 25–30 minutes until the pastry is golden and the filling nicely browned. Remove from the oven and serve warm or cold.

CRAGSIDE

When the inventor and industrialist William Armstrong made a nostalgic visit to Rothbury in 1863 as a break from the unrelenting pressures of his factory on the River Tyne, he determined to purchase what he could of the secluded Debdon Valley where he had so often wandered as a boy. A couple of watercolours showing tall chimneys belching smoke over factory buildings are the only direct reminders of the works which financed the rambling house set high above a ravine and buried in a thickly wooded hillside. But Cragside contains many other pointers to the genius of the man who built it and the world into which he was drawn. This was the earliest house in the world to be lit by electricity derived from water power; a mass of pipes connects a lake on the moors above to the generator sited on the estate.

Armstrong's activities are reflected too in the gradual transformation of the modest weekend retreat he had built in 1864–6. Shortly afterwards he engaged the architect Richard Norman Shaw, who over the next fifteen years turned Cragside into a country mansion and enriched it with some of his most original work. Shaw's grandest rooms were designed for important overseas clients. The King of Siam, the Shah of Persia and the Crown Prince of Afghanistan all slept in the monumental black walnut bed and a massive half-tester created for the guest chambers.

Even below stairs there is evidence of Armstrong's talents. The butler's pantry has an internal telephone, and in the kitchen itself there is a hydraulic spit and a service lift connecting with the basement.

Singin' Hinny

Makes 1 × 9in (22·5cm) round cake

12oz (350g) self-raising flour, sifted
1 teaspoon baking powder
2oz (50g) ground rice
1 teaspoon salt
2oz (50g) butter, softened

2oz (50g) caster sugar
3oz (75g) currants
5fl oz (150ml) double cream
5fl oz (150ml) milk

Preheat a griddle or a large, heavy frying pan to an even, moderate temperature. Mix together the flour, baking powder, ground rice and salt and rub in the fat until the mixture resembles fine breadcrumbs. Add the sugar and currants and mix well. Add the cream and milk and mix to a stiff dough. Knead lightly until smooth. On a lightly floured board, roll out to a circle 9in (22·5cm) in diameter and about ¼in (0·5cm) in thickness. Place on the griddle or pan and cook for 4–5 minutes on each side until golden. Serve hot or cold, cut into wedges and spread with butter and jam.

Sly Cake

Makes 8–10 pieces

12–14oz (350–400g) shortcrust
   pastry (see page 16)
6oz (175g) stoned dates, chopped
2oz (50g) raisins
2oz (50g) currants
2oz (50g) walnuts, chopped

2oz (50g) light or dark soft brown
   sugar
4 tablespoons water
2oz (50g) butter
1–2 tablespoons milk
2 tablespoons demerara sugar for
   dredging

Make the pastry according to the instructions on page 16 and chill for at least 15 minutes. Preheat the oven to gas mark 5/375°F/190°C. Grease a tin measuring approximately 9 × 4in (22·5 × 10cm). On a floured board, roll out half the pastry and use to line the base and sides of the tin. Put the dates, raisins, currants, walnuts, sugar, water and butter into a pan, bring to the boil and simmer for 10 minutes. Remove from the heat and allow to cool for a few minutes. Turn the mixture into the pastry case and spread evenly. Roll out the remaining pastry and lay over the fruit. Dampen the edges of the pastry with a little milk and pinch well together. Brush the top with milk, dredge with the demerara sugar and bake for 25–30 minutes until the pastry is golden. Remove from the oven and leave to cool in the tin. When cold, cut into pieces and remove carefully from the tin.

Yorkshire Curd Cheesecake

Makes 1 × 9in (22·5cm) round tart

4oz (100g) shortcrust pastry (see page 16)
8oz (225g) curd cheese
2oz (50g) caster sugar
2 eggs, beaten

the grated rind of half a lemon
the juice of 1 lemon
2 teaspoons cornflour
2 teaspoons double cream
1 tablespoon butter, melted

Make the pastry according to the instructions on page 16 and chill for at least 15 minutes. Preheat the oven to gas mark 5/375°F/190°C. Grease a 9in (22·5cm) loose-bottomed flan tin. On a lightly floured board, roll out the pastry and use to line the prepared tin. Bake blind for 15 minutes. Remove from the oven and reduce the oven temperature to gas mark 4/350°F/180°C. Blend together the curd cheese, sugar, beaten eggs, lemon rind and juice and beat until smooth. Blend the cornflour with the cream and fold into the cheese mixture with the melted butter. Pour into the pastry case and bake for 30 minutes until firm and golden. Remove from the oven and allow to cool in the tin.

EAST RIDDLESDEN HALL

Although W. S. Gilbert is said to have based the Bad Baronets in *Ruddigore* on the Murgatroyds of East Riddlesden, it seems the family does not entirely deserve its dubious reputation. Certainly the rich clothier James Murgatroyd who bought the estate in the 1630s was a respected local figure, and it is he who was largely responsible for the present house, its fine stonework now attractively darkened.

Absentee owners from the beginning of the nineteenth century ensured that this fine example of a seventeenth-century Yorkshire manor survived virtually unaltered. Almost empty when it was saved from dereliction in the early 1930s, East Riddlesden has been refurbished by the Trust. In the drawing-room there is a most unusual teapot in the form of a Chinese peach-shaped wine ewer. It is called the Cadogan teapot, as a certain Honourable Mrs Cadogan is said to have brought to England the original Chinese model which was adopted by the Rockingham factory in the early nineteenth century.

When brewing tea, the Chinese used tall, traditional wine ewers to hold the boiling water which was then poured on to tea leaves in small bowls. By the time these ewers were imported to Britain in the early seventeenth century, they had changed shape to become small, squat, broad-based teapots, and the narrow, elegant spout was wide enough not to clog with tea leaves. The earlier straight handle had been adapted to provide a curved one that fitted the fingers and enabled easier and safer pouring.

Carrot and Pineapple Cake

Makes 1 × 2lb (900g) loaf

1½ cups rice flour
1 cup caster sugar
½ teaspoon salt
½ teaspoon bicarbonate of soda
½ cup undrained crushed pineapple

1 cup grated carrot
½ cup corn or vegetable oil
2 eggs, beaten
½ teaspoon vanilla essence
½ cup walnuts, roughly chopped

Preheat the oven to gas mark 5/375°F/190°C. Grease and line a 2lb (900g) loaf tin. Mix together the flour, sugar, salt and bicarbonate of soda. Add the pineapple, carrot, oil, eggs, vanilla essence and walnuts and mix thoroughly. Turn into the prepared tin and bake for 1–1½ hours until a skewer comes out clean. Remove from the oven and leave to cool in the tin for a few minutes before turning out on to a wire rack to cool completely.

This cake contains no gluten and is thus excellent for anybody who cannot eat wheat flour. As it contains no fat, it is also low in cholesterol.

Iced Coffee and Cherry Tea Bread

Makes 1 × 2lb (900g) loaf

FOR THE CAKE
4oz (100g) margarine, softened
8oz (225g) self-raising flour, sifted
4oz (100g) light soft brown sugar
3oz (75g) walnuts, chopped
4oz (100g) glacé cherries, halved
½ teaspoon ground cinnamon

½ teaspoon mixed spice
2 eggs, beaten
2 teaspoons granulated coffee
mixed with 3 teaspoons boiling
water and allowed to cool

FOR THE ICING
8oz (225g) icing sugar, sifted
1 teaspoon granulated coffee mixed
with a little boiling water

boiling water to mix

Preheat the oven to gas mark 4/350°F/180°C. Grease and line a 2lb (900g) loaf tin. Rub the margarine into the flour until the mixture resembles fine breadcrumbs. Add the sugar, walnuts, cherries and spices and mix well. Add the beaten eggs and coffee essence and mix thoroughly so that all the ingredients are evenly distributed. Turn into the prepared tin and bake for 1–1½ hours until a skewer comes out clean.

Remove from the oven and leave to cool in the tin for at least 15 minutes before turning out on to a wire rack to cool completely. Make up the icing by mixing the icing sugar and coffee essence with enough boiling water to give a smooth, spreadable but not too runny consistency. When the loaf is cold, pour on the icing and leave to set.

Yorkshire Curd Tart

Makes 1 × 8in (20cm) round tart

6oz (175g) shortcrust pastry
  (see page 16)
2oz (50g) margarine, softened
2oz (50g) caster sugar
1 egg, beaten

2oz (50g) currants
4oz (100g) cottage cheese
2oz (50g) sponge or biscuit crumbs
the grated rind and juice of 1 lemon
½ teaspoon grated nutmeg

Make the pastry according to the instructions on page 16 and chill for at least 15 minutes. Preheat the oven to gas mark 5/375°F/190°C. Grease an 8in (20cm) round flan dish or tin. On a floured board, roll out the pastry to make a circle to fit the prepared tin or dish and use to line the base and sides. Beat together the margarine and sugar until light and fluffy. Add the beaten egg and beat hard. Add the currants, cottage cheese, sponge or biscuit crumbs, lemon juice and rind and the nutmeg and beat again. Turn into the pastry case, smooth and bake for 20-25 minutes until golden. Remove from the oven and serve warm or cold with thick cream.

FOUNTAINS ABBEY AND STUDLEY ROYAL

The ruins of the twelfth-century Fountains Abbey lie hidden away in the valley of the River Skell, the east end of the church dramatically framed by steep wooded slopes in the long vista upstream from the garden of Studley Royal. The enchanting formal water garden was the inspiration of John Aislabie, who inherited the Studley Royal Estate in 1699. An able and ambitious politician who rose to be Chancellor of the Exchequer, his meteoric career was brought to a sudden end in 1720 by his involvement in the South Sea Bubble which led to his expulsion from Parliament. Returning to Yorkshire, he devoted himself to the garden he had started in 1716, perhaps regarding it as a refuge from the world.

While John Aislabie was responsible for the beautiful naturalistic park surrounding his creation, the intentionally wild landscape below the lake, where the Skell plunges into a natural gorge, is still largely as conceived by his son William, one of the first examples of the

Picturesque style in England and a direct contrast with the formality of his father's water garden. The family used the garden and its buildings for such pleasures as tea parties, and for eating fruit and drinking sherbets in the Banqueting House. Beside the Octagon Tower are the remains of an outdoor kitchen used when meals were taken at this spot.

Daniel's Coffee and Drambuie Meringues

Makes 8 meringue nests

4 egg whites
10oz (275g) caster sugar
1 teaspoon cornflour
1 teaspoon vanilla essence
½ teaspoon white wine vinegar

10fl oz (300ml) double cream, whipped
3 tablespoons Drambuie
1 teaspoon finely ground coffee
8 walnut halves

Preheat the oven to gas mark ¼/225°F/110°C. Cover a baking tray with greaseproof paper. Whisk the egg whites with 4oz (100g) of the sugar until very stiff. Add another 4oz (100g) of sugar and whisk again. Add the cornflour, vanilla essence and vinegar and fold carefully in. Place the mixture in a large piping bag fitted with a ½in (1cm) star nozzle and pipe eight nests on to the greaseproof paper. Bake for 1 hour, then reduce the oven temperature to the lowest possible setting and bake for 4 hours more. Remove from the oven and leave to cool. If not needed immediately, place in an airtight container. When ready to use, mix together the whipped cream, Drambuie, coffee and the remaining 2oz (50g) of caster sugar (or more to taste) and place in a piping bag. Pipe the cream into the nests and decorate each with a half walnut.

These meringues are impressive enough to be served as a dessert at a dinner party or at a special tea party.

Old Peculier Fruit Cake

Makes 1 × 2lb (900g) loaf

4oz (100g) butter, softened
2oz (50g) light soft brown sugar
2oz (50g) caster sugar
2 eggs
3oz (75g) plain flour, sifted
3oz (75g) self-raising flour, sifted

4oz (100g) currants
2oz (50g) raisins
2oz (50g) sultanas
the juice and grated rind of 1 lemon
2¾ fl oz (70ml) Theakston's Old Peculier ale

Grease and line a 2lb (900g) loaf tin. Beat together the butter and sugar until light and fluffy. Add the eggs one at a time and beat well. Fold in the flour, dried fruit and lemon juice and rind. Add the Old Peculier and stir well. Turn into the prepared tin, cover and leave to stand overnight. The next day preheat the oven to gas mark 2/300°F/150°C. Bake the cake for 1¾–2 hours until a skewer comes out clean. Remove from the oven and turn out on to a wire rack to cool.

The addition of the Theakston's Old Peculier strong Yorkshire ale is what makes this cake so distinctive.

TREASURER'S HOUSE

Treasurer's House borders a narrow medieval cobbled street in the shadow of York Minster. Once attached to one of the wealthiest and most sought-after benefices in England, it was inhabited by successive treasurers of the cathedral from 1100 until the office was abolished under Henry VIII. Little remains of the medieval building or of the earlier structures suggested by the Roman column uncovered in the cellars.

The present elegant and roomy town house has had many and varied owners, including John Aislabie of Studley Royal (see page 101) and Dr Jacques Sterne, whose novelist nephew Laurence Sterne satirised the inward-looking society of the cathedral in *A Political Romance* (1759). In 1897 the house was acquired by Frank Green who was responsible for the contents which do so much to enhance its attractiveness. Amongst the items on display are some fine examples of Yorkshire pottery from Leeds and Castleford. There is also a Staffordshire teapot in the shape of a cauliflower, and a teapot on which the knob of the lid is in the shape of a lamb.

There is evidence that on 17 August 1923 Queen Mary took tea at Treasurer's House. She was staying near York with her daughter Princess Mary, Viscountess Lascelles, at Goldsborough Hall. The Queen was a great connoisseur of antiques and had spent much of her morning at Greenwood's, the long-established York antique dealers. History does not record her reaction to Frank Green's collection at Treasurer's House. Perhaps this is just as well; tradition has it that many country-house owners were rather nervous of Queen Mary's compliments because it was considered only good manners – and correct protocol – to offer the admired piece to Her Majesty.

Florence Nightingale said in 1869:
'There is nothing yet discovered which is a substitute to the Englishman for his cup of tea.'

Cut and Come Again Cake

Makes 1 × 8in (20cm) square cake

6oz (175g) margarine or butter, softened
10oz (275g) self-raising flour, sifted
6oz (175g) light soft brown sugar
4oz (100g) currants
6oz (175g) sultanas
2oz (50g) raisins
2oz (50g) mixed candied peel
a pinch of cinnamon
4 eggs, beaten
2 tablespoons milk

Preheat the oven to gas mark 3/325°F/160°C. Grease and line an 8in (20cm) square tin. Rub the margarine or butter into the flour until the mixture resembles fine breadcrumbs. Add the sugar, dried fruit and cinnamon and mix well. Add the beaten eggs and milk and mix to a soft consistency. Turn into the prepared tin and smooth the top. Bake for 1¼–1½ hours until a skewer comes out clean. Remove from the oven and turn out on to a wire rack to cool.

This is delicious served with Wensleydale cheese.

Wilfra Apple Cake

Makes 1 × 7 × 11in (17·5 × 27·5cm) tart

1lb (450g) shortcrust pastry (see page 16)
2lb (900g) cooking apples, peeled, cored and sliced
3–4oz (75–100g) granulated, demerara or soft brown sugar
2–3oz (50–75g) Wensleydale cheese, grated
milk or beaten egg to glaze

Make the pastry according to the instructions on page 16 and chill for at least 15 minutes. Preheat the oven to gas mark 5/375°F/190°C. Grease a 7 × 11in (17·5 × 27·5cm) Swiss roll tin. Cook the apples gently with the sugar until just soft. On a floured board, roll out half the pastry to make a rectangle to fit the tin and use to line the base and sides. Pour in the apples and spread evenly. Sprinkle the cheese over the apples. Roll out the remaining pastry and place on top of the cheese. Brush the edges with a little milk and seal well. Brush the top with milk or beaten egg and bake for 30–35 minutes until golden. Remove from the oven and allow to cool in the tin. When cold, cut into slabs and lift carefully from the tin.

A Hallowe'en Tea, clockwise from top left: Simone Sekers's fruit parkin (page 117); Eccles cakes (page 122), Cheshire souling cakes (page 110).

WALLINGTON

Many country houses are hidden behind walls or screens of trees, but there is nothing secluded about Wallington. This square stone building crowns a long slope of rough grass, majestically surveying the surrounding land and in full view of the public road through the park.

Wallington is largely the creation of Sir Walter Calverley Blackett, who in around 1738 commissioned the Northumbrian architect Daniel Garrett to remodel his grandfather's uncomfortable house. Oriental porcelain in the alcoves on either side of the fireplace in the saloon is part of a large and varied collection, much of it the dowry of Maria Wilson, who married into the family in 1791, just a few years after the house had passed to Sir Walter's nephew, Sir John Trevelyan. A bizarre Meissen tea set in the parlour features paintings of life-size insects nestling in the bottom of each cup.

Among other things, there are some fine examples of eighteenth-century Chinese and Japanese tea bowls. The Chinese did not put handles on their own teacups, because they drank their tea cool enough to render them unnecessary; the teacup with a handle is a European invention. In fact, China tea should never be drunk at a temperature which requires a handle on a cup, as the flavour is best sampled at a few degrees above blood heat.

Biscuits, clockwise from top left: Grantham gingerbreads (page 80); orange crisps (page 107), Melbourne wakes cakes (page 84); Linzer biscuits (page 106).

Linzer Biscuits

Makes approximately
25 double biscuits

10oz (275g) self-raising flour, sifted
a good pinch of ground cinnamon
a good pinch of ground cloves
8oz (225g) margarine, softened

6oz (175g) caster sugar
1 egg, beaten
5-6 tablespoons raspberry or
* apricot jam*

Preheat the oven to gas mark 3/325°F/160°C. Grease two or three baking trays. Mix together all the ingredients except the jam to make a soft dough. Knead gently until smooth. Roll out on a floured board to a thickness of ¼in (0·5cm) and cut out circles using a 2in (5cm) cutter. Using an apple corer or a very small cutter, cut a small circle from the middle of each round and re-roll the dough to make more biscuits. Place on the prepared trays, allowing space for the biscuits to spread, and bake for 10-15 minutes until golden. Remove from the oven and leave to cool on the trays for 5 minutes before lifting on to a wire rack to cool completely. When cold, sandwich together with the jam and store in an airtight container for 1-2 days before eating.

If you don't have time to roll and cut the dough, form the mixture into balls and place on the trays. Flatten with the prongs of a fork and don't worry about making the hole in the middle.

Melting Moments

Makes 20 biscuits

5oz (150g) sugar
6oz (175g) margarine, softened
8oz (225g) plain flour, sifted
3 teaspoons baking powder

1½ oz (40g) shredded coconut
1 teaspoon vanilla essence
10 glacé cherries, halved

Preheat the oven to gas mark 3/325°F/160°C. Grease two baking trays. Beat together the sugar and margarine until light and fluffy. Add the flour, baking powder, coconut and vanilla essence and mix thoroughly. Form the mixture into balls weighing approximately 1oz (25g) each and place on the prepared trays, leaving plenty of room for the biscuits to spread. Flatten with the palm of the hand and place a half cherry in the middle of each. Bake for 15-20 minutes until golden. Remove from the oven and leave to cool on the trays for 5 minutes before lifting on to a wire rack to cool completely.

Orange Crisps

Makes approximately
24 biscuits

5oz (150g) margarine, softened
5oz (150g) caster or granulated
  sugar
1 egg yolk
8oz (225g) plain flour, sifted
2 teaspoons baking powder

the grated rind and juice of half a
  small orange
1 egg white, beaten
4oz (100g) caster sugar for
  dredging

Preheat the oven to gas mark 5/375°F/190°C. Grease two or three baking trays. Beat together the margarine and sugar until light and fluffy. Add the egg yolk, flour, baking powder and orange rind and juice. Mix thoroughly to a stiff paste and knead until smooth. On a lightly floured board, roll out to a thickness of ¼in (0·5cm) and cut into rounds using a 2½in (6cm) cutter. Place on the prepared trays, leaving room for the biscuits to spread, brush the top of each with beaten egg white, dredge with caster sugar and bake for 10 minutes until pale golden. Remove from the oven and leave to cool for 5 minutes on the trays before lifting on to a wire rack to cool completely.

These biscuits are also excellent made with lemon juice and rind instead of orange.

Regional Specialities

Fat Rascals

Makes 7-8 biscuits

8oz (225g) plain flour, sifted
a pinch of salt
4oz (100g) butter, softened
1½ oz (40g) caster sugar

2oz (50g) currants
2-3fl oz (50-75ml) milk and
  water mixed
caster sugar for dredging

Preheat the oven to gas mark 6/400°F/200°C. Grease a baking tray. Mix together the flour and salt and rub in the butter. Add the sugar and currants and mix. Add enough milk and water to give a firm dough. On a floured board, roll out to a thickness of ½in (1cm) and cut out circles using a 3in (7·5cm) cutter. Place on the prepared tray, dredge with caster sugar and bake for 20-25 minutes until pale golden. Remove from the oven and lift carefully on to a wire rack to cool.

Ripon Christmas Bread

Makes 2 × 2lb (900g) loaves

FOR THE BASIC BREAD DOUGH

2lb (900g) plain flour, sifted
2 teaspoons salt
1oz (25g) fresh yeast
1 teaspoon caster sugar

4oz (100g) lard or margarine,
   softened
1 pint (600ml) milk, warmed

FOR THE ADDITIONAL FLAVOURING

6oz (175g) lard, softened and cut
   into small pieces
4oz (100g) raisins
2oz (50g) mixed candied peel

4oz (100g) granulated or caster
   sugar
8oz (225g) currants
½ teaspoon allspice

First make the basic bread dough. Mix together the flour and salt. Cream the yeast with the sugar. Rub the fat into the flour, add the yeast and warm milk and mix to a light dough. Knead well with floured hands until smooth. Place the dough in a bowl and stand in a warm place for 1½–2 hours until doubled in size. Grease two 2lb (900g) loaf tins. Mix together all the additional ingredients and work into the dough until all are evenly distributed. Divide the mixture between the tins and leave in a warm place until the dough almost reaches the top of the tins. Meanwhile heat the oven to gas mark 3/325°F/160°C. When the loaves are well risen, bake for approximately 2 hours until golden and firm. Remove from the oven and turn out on to a wire rack to cool. Serve warm or cold with butter.

In most areas of Britain in the past, large batches of fruit loaves were baked at Christmas ready to feed the family and any visitors who called at the house between Christmas and New Year.

Scarborough Muffins

Makes 10 muffins

14oz (400g) plain flour, sifted
a pinch of salt
10fl oz (300ml) milk

½oz (15g) fresh yeast
1 egg

Grease two baking trays. Mix together the flour and salt. Warm the milk and stir into the yeast. Beat the egg and add to the milk. Pour into the flour and blend well to give a soft dough. Knead lightly. On a floured board, roll out to a thickness of ½in (1cm) and cut into round cakes with a 3in (7·5cm) cutter. Place on the prepared trays and leave in a warm place for 1 hour until well risen. Meanwhile heat the oven to gas mark 6/400°F/200°C. When the muffins are well risen, bake for 10 minutes until golden. Remove from the oven and serve hot or warm with butter.

Muffins have been a favourite for breakfast and tea since Victorian times. Each region has its own recipe and this one makes a light, soft sponge that is excellent with cheese or preserves.

The North-West

The north-west region is very rich in traditional speciality baking. Cheshire and the town of Chester itself have tarts and souling cakes, which were originally made for All Souls' Day festivities on 2 November, and Cheshire cheese makes delicious scones. Manchester has its own tart filled with jam and a brandy and breadcrumb topping. Lancaster is known for its lemon tart, but probably the best-known Lancashire treat is the Eccles cake. Over the centuries, several regions of Britain have developed their own versions of this fruit-filled pastry. Oxfordshire's Banbury cakes are famous; less well known is that in Coventry triangular God cakes were traditionally given by godparents to their godchildren on New Year's Day to represent the Holy Trinity. Recipes for the filling have varied over the years, but most contain currants and spices, and sometimes rum or brandy. Eccles cakes are thought to be a descendant of cakes and loaves made as an offering at pagan and early Christian festivals. The word 'eccles' means church, and the cakes continued to be made for the annual wakes in the town of Eccles.

Cumbria, like Yorkshire, is renowned for its gingerbreads and parkins, the most famous being Grasmere gingerbread from the Lake District. Each year a fair is held at Grasmere on the Saturday nearest to St Oswald's Day on 5 August. After a special church service, a procession leads to Church Field where in the past wrestling matches took place. Today there are sports competitions and all the children receive a piece of gingerbread. Parkins are traditionally a Hallowe'en speciality and probably derive from the pagan practice of baking oatmeal and spice cakes for celebrations marking the beginning of winter. In Lancashire the cakes were called Har cakes after the god Har, and in Derbyshire they were named after Thor, the Scandinavian god of thunder, war and agriculture. The cakes were sometimes referred to as 'tharve' cakes (the hearth cake), as they were cooked on a bakestone on an open kitchen fire.

DUNHAM MASSEY

Dunham Massey is an attractive, long, low, red-brick building set around two courtyards and still protected by the medieval moat that embraced the earlier Tudor house. The sombre, low-ceilinged, oak-lined chapel, made out of two rooms in 1655, and the magnificent collection of Huguenot silver are both reflections of the Booth family's ardent

Protestantism. The exceptional Edwardian interiors were commissioned over two centuries later by William Grey, 9th Earl of Stamford, whose family acquired the estate through marriage.

In a small room known as the tea-room, possibly so called because the rare tea and coffee tables and some of the family silver were kept here, there are two large caddies on show. They are Japanned metal canisters inlaid with mother of pearl which were probably used originally to store large quantities of tea which then replenished smaller caddies. There are several ornate tea caddies around the house on mantelshelves or side tables; this is, of course, where they would have been kept, rather than in the kitchen. The caddies would be locked and strategically sited in the dining- or drawing-room so that the lady of the house could brew the beverage herself when her guests arrived for afternoon tea.

In the eighteenth century it was fashionable to serve tea, bread and butter to guests after evening dinner. Everyone would retire to the drawing-room where the tea table was set out ready. The tea-making equipment was brought in by a servant, the hostess would brew the tea and then the evening's conversation could begin. The first tea tables were imported from the East Indies at the end of the seventeenth century; at the beginning of the eighteenth century English cabinetmakers started to make ornate copies, mainly from walnut and mahogany. Most tables stood on curving cabriole legs that ended in plain ball and claw feet; they had rectangular, octagonal or round tops with a raised rim running round the edge to prevent tea ware from being knocked to the floor.

Cheshire Souling Cakes

Makes approximately 26 cakes

12oz (350g) plain flour, sifted
½ teaspoon ground cinnamon
½ teaspoon mixed spice
a pinch of nutmeg

6oz (175g) caster sugar
6oz (175g) margarine, softened
1 egg, beaten
1½ teaspoons white wine vinegar

Preheat the oven to gas mark 4/350°F/180°C. Grease two baking trays. Mix together all the dry ingredients and rub in the margarine. Add the beaten egg and vinegar and mix to a soft dough. Knead gently until smooth. On a lightly floured board, roll out to a thickness of ¼in (0·5cm) and cut into rounds with a 3in (7·5cm) cutter. Place on the prepared trays and bake for 15–20 minutes until lightly browned. Remove from the oven and leave to cool on the trays for a few minutes before lifting carefully on to a wire rack to cool completely.

Souling cakes were baked for All Souls' Day when children went round the villages begging for sustenance. The cakes are thought to have descended from food left in graves for the dead in pagan days.

Lancaster Lemon Tart

Makes 1 × 8in (20cm)
round tart

6oz (175g) shortcrust pastry
  (see page 16)
5–6oz (150–175g) lemon curd
4oz (100g) margarine, softened
4oz (100g) caster sugar

2 eggs, beaten
3 teaspoons lemon juice
3oz (75g) self-raising flour, sifted
1oz (25g) ground almonds

Make the pastry according to the instructions on page 16 and chill for at least 15 minutes. Preheat the oven to gas mark 4/350°F/180°C. Grease an 8in (20cm) loose-bottomed round flan tin. On a floured board, roll out the pastry and use to line the tin. Spread the lemon curd over the base. Beat together the margarine and sugar until pale and fluffy. Gradually add the beaten eggs and the lemon juice and beat well. Add the flour and ground almonds and fold in with a metal spoon. Spread the mixture over the lemon curd and smooth out. Bake for 35 minutes, then reduce the oven temperature to gas mark 2/300°F/150°C and bake for 10–15 minutes more until the sponge springs back when lightly pressed. Remove from the oven and leave to cool in the tin. When cold, cut into pieces.

Manchester Tart

Makes 1 × 8in (20cm)
round tart

6oz (175g) flaky pastry
  (see page 15)
3–4 tablespoons raspberry or
  strawberry jam
the rind of 1 lemon, cut into strips
10fl oz (300ml) milk

2oz (50g) fresh breadcrumbs
2oz (50g) butter, softened
2 eggs, separated
3oz (75g) caster sugar
1 tablespoon brandy
caster sugar for dredging

Make the pastry according to the instructions on page 15 and chill for at least 45 minutes. Preheat the oven to gas mark 5/375°F/190°C. Grease and line an 8in (20cm) round pie dish or loose-bottomed round tin. On a floured board, roll out the pastry and use to line the prepared tin. Spread the jam over the base. Put the lemon rind and milk into a pan and bring to the boil. Remove from the heat and strain on to the breadcrumbs. Leave to stand for 5 minutes. Add the butter, egg yolks, 1oz (25g) of the sugar and the brandy and beat well. Pour into the pastry case and bake for 45 minutes. Meanwhile whisk the egg whites until stiff and fold in the remaining 2oz (50g) of the sugar. Remove the tart from the oven and spread the meringue over the filling. Dredge with caster sugar and bake for a further 15 minutes until the meringue is brown. Remove from the oven and leave to cool. Serve cold with cream.

LITTLE MORETON HALL

The prosperous Moretons of Little Moreton Hall were gentleman farmers, profiting like many of their kind from the sale of land following the Dissolution of the Monasteries. Their timber-framed, moated house was originally only two storeys tall, the upper floor jettied out over the lower. Between about 1570 and 1580, when the size of the estate was doubled, the substantial long gallery was added to the south wing, giving the house its curiously top-heavy appearance.

Apart from three pieces, all the original contents have disappeared and the rooms are shown unfurnished. As a result, nothing distracts from the remarkable nature of the building itself, which seems to have been devised to display the full range of the joiners' and carpenters' art. The confidence and pride of the carpenter who carried out extensive work in 1559 is proclaimed in the inscription he left on one of the bay windows: 'Rycharde Dale Carpeder made thies windous by the grac of god.'

The interior is a warren, one room leading into another, some little more than cupboards, others grand chambers with fine chimneypieces and panelling, four staircases linking the different levels. A seventeenth-century 'cubborde of boxes' in the hall was probably used to store precious spices and would have been kept locked by the lady of the house. She would have dished them out to the cook in very careful measures for use in sweet and savoury recipes.

Fruit Scones

Makes 14–16 scones

1lb (450g) self-raising flour, sifted
a pinch of salt .
½ teaspoon baking powder
4oz (100g) margarine, softened
1½ tablespoons caster sugar
1½ tablespoons sultanas
just under 10fl oz (300ml) milk

Preheat the oven to gas mark 7/425°F/220°C. Grease two baking trays. Mix together the flour, salt and baking powder and rub in the margarine. Add the sugar and sultanas and mix together with enough milk to give a soft dough. On a floured board, roll out to a thickness of ¾in (1·5cm) and cut into rounds using a 2½in (6cm) cutter. Place on the prepared trays and bake for 13–15 minutes until golden and firm. Remove from the oven and lift on to a wire rack to cool. Serve warm or cold with butter.

Mocha Slices

Makes 20 slices

FOR THE BASE
8oz (225g) margarine
8oz (225g) self-raising flour, sifted
2oz (50g) cocoa powder, sifted

8oz (225g) caster or granulated sugar
5oz (150g) porridge oats

FOR THE ICING
2oz (50g) margarine
8oz (225g) icing sugar, sifted

1 tablespoon granulated coffee dissolved in 1 tablespoon boiling water

Preheat the oven to gas mark 4/350°F/180°C. Grease a 7 × 11in (17·5 × 27·5cm) Swiss roll tin. Melt the margarine in a pan. Mix together the flour, cocoa powder, sugar and oats. Add the melted margarine and mix thoroughly. Turn into the prepared tin and press well down. Smooth the top and bake for 10 minutes exactly. Remove from the oven and leave to cool. To make the icing, melt the margarine, add the icing sugar and coffee essence and beat together. Spread over the cooled cake and make a pattern with the prongs of a fork. Leave to set. When set, cut into slices.

MOSELEY OLD HALL

In the early hours of 8 September 1651, five days after the Royalist defeat at the Battle of Worcester, Charles II disguised as a woodcutter arrived at Moseley Old Hall. He was met by Thomas Whitgreave, the owner, and his chaplain; together they escorted the King to the priest's room, now known as the King's Room. Here he was shown the hiding place which was to serve him well when the Parliamentarians came to the house two days later. The night after this unwelcome visit, the King mounted a horse and rode away disguised as a serving man on the first leg of his long and hazardous journey to safety on the Continent.

Visitors to Moseley Old Hall retrace Charles's route on that fateful night 350 years ago. Although the façades of the Elizabethan house were faced in brick in the nineteenth century and the mullioned windows have been replaced by casements, much of the original panelling and timber-framing inside the house still survives, and heavy oak seventeenth-century furniture, including the bed on which Charles slept, and contemporary portraits of the King and those who helped him, all contribute to an authentic atmosphere.

It was Charles's wife, Catharine of Braganza, who was largely responsible for introducing tea to the British aristocracy in 1662, when she brought with her a chest of tea as part of her dowry. If Charles had been captured by the Roundheads in 1651, he might not have lived to marry Catharine and tea might not have become such an important part of British life.

Orange Tea Bread

Makes 1 × 2lb (900g) loaf

8oz (225g) self-raising flour (white or wholemeal), sifted
3oz (75g) butter, softened
3oz (75g) caster sugar
2oz (50g) walnuts, roughly chopped
1 large egg, beaten

2 oranges (the grated rind of both, the juice from one and the other left whole)
2 tablespoons caster sugar for sprinkling

Preheat the oven to gas mark 4/350°F/180°C. Grease and line a 2lb (900g) loaf tin. Rub the butter into the flour until the mixture resembles fine breadcrumbs. Stir in the sugar and walnuts. Add the egg, orange rind and juice and beat well. Turn into the prepared tin. Holding the remaining orange over the tin so as to catch any juice, remove the skin and pith and divide into segments. Arrange over the top of the cake and sprinkle with the caster sugar. Bake for 1¼–1½ hours until a skewer comes out clean. Remove from the oven and leave to cool in the tin.

Seventeenth-Century Honey Cake

Makes 1 × 2lb (900g) loaf or 7in (17·5cm) round cake

FOR THE CAKE
6oz (175g) butter, softened
6oz (175g) caster sugar
3 eggs, beaten
6oz (175g) white or wholemeal self-raising flour, sifted

1 teaspoon baking powder
1 tablespoon clear honey
a few drops of almond essence

FOR THE TOPPING
1 dessertspoon clear honey

the juice of 1 lemon

FOR THE ICING
5oz (150g) cream cheese
the juice of half a lemon

6oz (175g) icing sugar, sifted

Preheat the oven to gas mark 4/350°F/180°C. Grease and line a 2lb (900g) loaf tin or a 7in (17·5cm) round tin. Beat together the butter and sugar until light and fluffy. Add the eggs, flour and baking powder and beat hard. Add the honey and almond essence and continue beating for 1–2 minutes. Turn into the prepared tin and bake for 1–1¼ hours until a skewer comes out clean. (After half an hour, cover the top with a double layer of greaseproof paper as the cake tends to darken quite quickly.) Remove from the oven. Mix together the honey and lemon juice and pour over the top. Leave to cool in the tin, then turn out. Beat together the cream cheese, lemon juice and icing sugar and spread over the cooled cake. Make a pattern with the prongs of a fork and then serve.

Tafferty Tart

Makes 1 × 8in (20cm)
round tart

FOR THE TART
8oz (225g) shortcrust pastry
 (see page 16)
the grated rind of 2 lemons
the juice of half a lemon and a little
 of the flesh

5oz (150g) caster sugar
8 large cooking apples, peeled,
 cored and sliced
1–2oz (25–50g) butter

FOR THE ICING
4oz (100g) icing sugar, sifted
1 teaspoon lemon juice

1 dessertspoon milk

Make the pastry according to the instructions on page 16 and chill for at least 15 minutes. Preheat the oven to gas mark 8/450°F/230°C. Grease an 8in (20cm) round flan dish or tin. On a floured board, roll out two-thirds of the pastry to make a circle to fit the prepared tin. Mix together the lemon rind, juice, flesh and sugar. Arrange the apple slices in layers in the pastry case, sprinkling some of the lemon and sugar mixture on each layer. Cut the butter into small pieces and arrange on top of the apples. Roll out the remaining portion of pastry to make a circle to fit the top of the tart and use to cover the apples. Wet the edges with a little milk or water and press well together. Make a hole in the middle to allow steam to escape. Bake for 10 minutes, then reduce the oven temperature to gas mark 5/375°F/190°C and bake for a further 25–30 minutes until the pastry is golden and firm. Meanwhile mix together the ingredients for the icing. Remove the tart from the oven and immediately pour the icing over the top. Put back into the oven and bake for 5 minutes more. (The icing becomes opaque.) Remove from the oven and serve warm or cold with cream.

Why do they always put mud into coffee on board steamers?
Why does the tea generally taste of boiled boots?

William Makepeace Thackeray (1811-63)

QUARRY BANK MILL

The cotton industry was marked by a watershed in 1783. The patents protecting Richard Arkwright's revolutionary new spinning machine were challenged and overthrown, opening the way for a huge expansion in factory-produced yarn. One of the first to take advantage of the new opportunities was the young Samuel Greg, the son of a prosperous Belfast merchant, who found a suitable site for a water-powered mill in the isolated Bollin Valley some ten miles south of Manchester and established a new cotton-spinning business here in 1784. As the mill prospered it was enlarged, and a little village complete with school, shop and chapel was built in the early nineteenth century to house the growing labour force. Remarkably, the buildings survive virtually unchanged.

The Greg family never lost the humanitarian interests which are so evident in the layout of the village. Behind each red-brick cottage are the remains of a privy, a great luxury at a time when such facilities were usually shared between several families. Near the mill is the apprentice house, built as early as 1790 to accommodate the children who made up about a third of the workforce. The staple diet of an average Manchester worker was potatoes and wheaten bread, washed down by tea or coffee. The Comte de la Rochefoucauld, while touring England in 1784, reported: 'Throughout the whole of England the drinking of tea is general. You have it twice a day and though the expense is considerable, the humblest peasant has his tea twice a day just like the rich man.'

Most British workmen today drink their tea with milk and sugar. Sugar first became popular in tea at the end of the seventeenth century, and milk or cream in the mid-eighteenth century. Cream and milk were usually served hot in silver jugs; the ceramics industry in Britain had not yet mastered a method to make porcelain, and their stoneware and earthenware could not withstand the temperature of boiling milk. Later it became fashionable to serve milk in a jug shaped like a dairy cow, but more elegant creamers were similar to sauce boats.

Apple Cinnamon Cake

Makes 1 × 8in (20cm) round cake

FOR THE CAKE

7oz (200g) self-raising flour, sifted
3oz (75g) caster sugar

5oz (150g) margarine, softened
1 large egg

FOR THE FILLING

2 cooking apples, peeled, cored and sliced
2 tablespoons granulated sugar

2 teaspoons ground cinnamon
2 tablespoons strawberry or apricot jam

Preheat the oven to gas mark 4/350°F/180°C. Grease and line an 8in (20cm) round tin. Sieve the flour into a mixing bowl. Add the sugar, margarine and unbeaten egg. Using a wooden spoon, mix the ingredients gently for about 2 minutes until thoroughly combined. Turn two-thirds of the mixture into the prepared tin and smooth. Lay the apples on top and sprinkle with the granulated sugar and cinnamon. Drop spoonfuls of the remaining cake mixture on top of the apples but do not spread. Place teaspoonfuls of jam in between the cake mixture. Bake for 1 hour until golden and firm. Remove from the oven and allow to cool in the tin.

Lakeland Coconut Tart

Makes 1 × 8in (20cm) round tart

6oz (175g) shortcrust pastry
  (see page 16)
3-4 tablespoons strawberry or
  raspberry jam
4oz (100g) margarine

2oz (50g) caster sugar
2 level tablespoons golden syrup
8oz (225g) shredded coconut
2 eggs, beaten

Make the pastry according to the instructions on page 16 and chill for at least 15 minutes. Preheat the oven to gas mark 5/375°F/190°C. Grease an 8in (20cm) round flan tin or a deep pie plate. On a floured board, roll out the pastry and use to line the prepared tin. Spread the jam over the pastry base. Melt together the margarine, sugar and syrup and stir in the coconut and beaten eggs. Turn into the pastry case and bake in the middle of the oven for 30 minutes until golden. (This tart browns and burns easily, so cover with foil after the first 10 minutes of baking time.) Remove from the oven and leave to cool in the tin.

Simone Sekers's Fruit Parkin

Makes 24 slices

15fl oz (400ml) water
4oz (100g) lard
6oz (175g) light or dark soft brown
  sugar
8oz (225g) golden syrup
8oz (225g) black treacle
4oz (100g) currants
2oz (50g) mixed candied peel

1lb (450g) plain flour, sifted
8oz (225g) medium oatmeal
2 teaspoons mixed spice
1½ teaspoons ground ginger
a pinch of salt and 1 teaspoon
  bicarbonate of soda dissolved
  in a little water

Preheat the oven to gas mark 3/325°F/160°C. Grease and line a deep roasting tin measuring approximately 12 × 8in (30 × 20cm). Warm together the water, lard, sugar, syrup and treacle until melted. When cool, add all the other ingredients and mix thoroughly so that all are evenly distributed. Turn into the prepared tin and bake for 1-1½ hours until firm and well risen. Remove from the oven and leave to cool in the tin. When cold, cut into squares or slices.

RUFFORD OLD HALL

Like his father, grandfather and great-grandfather before him, Sir Thomas Hesketh married an heiress. Certainly no expense was spared on the half-timbered manor house he built in around 1420, establishing the family seat for the next 350 years. Although only the great hall survives in its original form, what remains speaks eloquently of wealth and position. The great hall was built to be admired, crowned by a fanciful hammer-beam roof.

A massive, intricately carved movable wooden screen takes the place of the more usual partition in houses of this date, separating the hall from the traditional screens passage. This deliberately theatrical set piece must have delighted William Shakespeare if there is truth in the legend that he performed here while in the Heskeths' service. A long refectory table, richly carved oak chests and pieces from the Hesketh collection of arms and armour add to the house's atmosphere.

There are a number of teapots on show around the house, including, in the kitchen, one with a tiny replica teapot as the knob on the lid. There are also two huge Victorian specimens which measure about fifteen inches high and eighteen inches across from the end of the spout to the handle; these were used for serving punch when they outgrew their original function. In the drawing-room there is a large ornate teapoy which belonged to the Hesketh family and which bears their crest. A teapoy was a small individual table placed beside a seated guest to hold his or her teacup and saucer. It was similar in design to a tea table but stood only two feet high. By 1800 the word had come to mean a table that had an integral caddy.

Cherry and Almond Scones

Makes 20 scones

1lb (450g) self-raising flour, sifted
½ teaspoon baking powder
4oz (100g) margarine, softened
3oz (75g) caster sugar

3oz (75g) glacé cherries, roughly chopped
1 egg, beaten
a few drops of almond essence
6–7fl oz (175–200ml) milk

Preheat the oven to gas mark 4/350°F/180°C. Grease two baking trays. Mix together the flour and baking powder and rub in the margarine. Add the sugar, cherries, beaten egg, almond essence and enough milk to give a soft but not sticky dough. Knead lightly until smooth. On a floured board, roll out to a thickness of ½in (1cm) and cut out rounds using a 2in (5cm) cutter. Place on the prepared trays and bake for 20–25 minutes until well risen, firm and golden. Remove from the oven and lift on to a wire rack to cool. Serve with butter or clotted cream and jam.

Chocolate Orange Drizzle Cake

Makes 1 × 2lb (900g) loaf or 7in (17·5cm) round cake

FOR THE CAKE
6oz (175g) margarine, softened
6oz (175g) caster sugar
3 large eggs
the grated rind of 2 oranges
6oz (175g) self-raising flour, sifted
2 tablespoons milk

FOR THE TOPPING
the juice of 2 oranges
4oz (100g) granulated sugar
2oz (50g) milk or plain chocolate

Preheat the oven to gas mark 4/350°F/180°C. Grease and line a 2lb (900g) loaf tin or a 7in (17·5cm) round tin. Cream together the margarine and sugar until light and fluffy. Add the eggs, one at a time, and beat well. Add the grated orange rind, flour and milk and fold in with a metal spoon. Turn into the prepared tin, smooth the top and bake for 30–40 minutes until a skewer comes out clean. Remove from the oven and leave to cool in the tin. When cool, score the top of the cake lightly with a sharp knife. Put the orange juice and granulated sugar into a pan and heat gently until the sugar has dissolved. Bring to the boil and boil for 1–2 minutes. Pour over the cake. When all the juice has soaked in, carefully remove the cake from the tin. Melt the chocolate and pour over the top. Make a pattern with the prongs of a fork and leave to set.

Streusal Crunchy Cake

Makes 1 × 7in (17·5cm) round cake

FOR THE CAKE
5oz (150g) self-raising flour, sifted
5oz (150g) light soft brown sugar
6oz (175g) margarine, softened
3 eggs, beaten

FOR THE FILLING AND TOPPING
2 tablespoons muesli cereal
   (Jordans Original or similar)
1 tablespoon light soft brown sugar
1 teaspoon ground cinnamon
2oz (50g) walnuts, roughly chopped

Preheat the oven to gas mark 4/350°F/180°C. Grease and line a 7in (17·5cm) loose-bottomed round tin. Place the flour, sugar, margarine and eggs together in a bowl and beat for 2 minutes. Turn half the mixture into the prepared tin and press down. Mix together the ingredients for the filling and topping and sprinkle two-thirds over the cake. Spread the remaining cake mixture on top and smooth. Sprinkle the remaining muesli mixture over the top and bake for 20–25 minutes until firm and browned. Remove from the oven and leave to cool in the tin.

WORDSWORTH HOUSE

Although the adult William Wordsworth is mainly connected with the southern Lakes, his formative years were spent in the north of the Lake District, in the little market town of Cockermouth on the River Derwent where his father was agent to Sir James Lowther. The Georgian house where he was born on 7 April 1770, almost two years before his sister Dorothy, stands at the west end of the main street, its garden stretching down to the river and only a stone's throw from the ruined castle from which William derived so much inspiration.

Seven of the modest family rooms are furnished in eighteenth-century style, as the Wordsworths might have had them, and include some pieces which belonged to the poet in later life – his painted bookshelves, his sofa, his longcase clock and his porcelain inkstand. Southey's fine Georgian walnut chairs grace the drawing-room, which is hung with early prints of the Lake District.

Dorothy Wordsworth's Favourite Cake

Makes 1 × 2lb (900g) loaf

6oz (175g) margarine, softened
6oz (175g) caster sugar
3 eggs
3 teaspoons caraway seeds
8oz (225g) plain flour, sifted
1 teaspoon baking powder
a pinch of salt
1 tablespoon ground almonds
1 tablespoon milk

Preheat the oven to gas mark 4/350°F/180°C. Grease and line a 2lb (900g) loaf tin. Beat together the margarine and sugar until light and fluffy, then beat in the eggs. Add the caraway seeds, flour, baking powder, salt, almonds and milk and mix carefully so that all the ingredients are evenly distributed. Turn into the prepared tin and bake for 45-55 minutes until a skewer comes out clean. Remove from the oven and leave to cool in the tin.

Eighteenth-Century Pepper Cake

Makes 1 × 9in (22·5cm) round cake

1lb (450g) plain flour, sifted
1 teaspoon baking powder
4oz (100g) margarine or butter, softened
8oz (225g) caster sugar
4oz (100g) currants
4oz (100g) raisins
1oz (25g) mixed candied peel
½ teaspoon ground cloves
½ teaspoon ground ginger
½ teaspoon black pepper
8oz (225g) black treacle
2 eggs, beaten

Preheat the oven to gas mark 2/300°F/150°C. Grease and line a 9in (22·5cm) round deep cake tin. Mix together the flour and baking powder and rub in the margarine or butter until the mixture resembles fine breadcrumbs. Add all the other ingredients and mix to a thick batter. Turn into the prepared tin and bake for 2-2¼ hours until a skewer comes out clean. Remove from the oven and leave to cool in the tin for 15 minutes before turning out on to a wire rack to cool completely. When cool, wrap in foil or cling film and store for a few days before using.

The cake may be coated with marzipan and iced with a plain white icing made with 6-8oz (175-225g) icing sugar, sifted and mixed with 1-2 tablespoons cold water or lemon juice.

Featherlight Wholewheat Cake

Makes 1 × 7in (17·5cm) round cake

FOR THE CAKE
4oz (100g) margarine, softened
4oz (100g) light or dark soft brown sugar
2 egg yolks

1 tablespoon cold water
4oz (100g) wholewheat self-raising flour, sifted
2 egg whites

FOR THE FILLING AND ICING
7oz (200g) low-fat cream cheese
2oz (50g) icing sugar, sifted

3oz (75g) walnuts, chopped

TO DECORATE
9 half walnuts

Preheat the oven to gas mark 4/350°F/180°C. Grease two 7in (17·5cm) round sandwich tins. Beat together the margarine and sugar until light and fluffy. Beat together the egg yolks and water, add to the mixture and beat hard. Fold in the flour. Whisk the egg whites until stiff, then fold in. Turn into the prepared tins and smooth. Bake for 20–25 minutes until well risen and golden. Remove from the oven and leave to cool in the tins for 5 minutes, then turn out on to a wire rack to cool completely. Mean-while beat together the ingredients for the filling until light and fluffy. When the cake is cold, spread half of the mixture on one cake and place the other cake on top. Ice with the remaining mixture and decorate with half walnuts.

Regional Specialities

Eccles Cakes

Makes 12 cakes

8-10oz (225-275g) flaky pastry
  (see page 15)
1oz (25g) butter, softened
1oz (25g) light soft brown sugar
1oz (25g) mixed candied peel

3oz (75g) currants
1 teaspoon mixed spice
a little milk or water
1 egg white, beaten
2 tablespoons caster sugar

Make the pastry according to the instructions on page 15 and chill for at least 1 hour. Grease two baking trays. On a floured board, roll out the pastry to a thickness of approximately ¼in (0·5cm) and cut out circles using a 4in (10cm) cutter (a cup or bowl will do very nicely if you do not have a big enough cutter). Mix together the butter and brown sugar, add the dried fruit and spice and mix well. Place a teaspoonful of the mixture on each pastry circle. Dampen the edges of the pastry with a little milk or water, gather the edges together and seal well. Turn the cakes over so that the joins are underneath. Roll each one out so that the currants just show through the pastry and place on the prepared trays. Chill for 10-15 minutes. Meanwhile heat the oven to gas mark 8/450°F/230°C. Make two or three slits on the top of each cake, brush with beaten egg white and dredge with caster sugar. Bake for 10-15 minutes until crisp and golden. Remove from the oven and lift carefully on to a wire rack to cool.

Grasmere Gingerbread

Makes 16 pieces

10oz (275g) plain flour, sifted
1 teaspoon ground ginger
½ teaspoon ground cinnamon
a pinch of salt
4oz (100g) stoned dates, chopped
5oz (150g) black treacle

3oz (75g) butter
4oz (100g) dark soft brown sugar
1 egg, beaten
¾ teaspoon bicarbonate of soda
  dissolved in 3 tablespoons milk

Preheat the oven to gas mark 3/325°F/170°C. Grease and line a 10in (25cm) square tin. Mix together the flour, ginger, cinnamon and salt. Add the dates. Melt the treacle, butter and sugar together on a gentle heat, then leave to cool for a few minutes. Add the flour mixture and mix thoroughly. Add the beaten egg, bicarbonate of soda and milk and blend well to a fairly wet consistency, adding a little more milk if too dry. Turn into the prepared tin and bake for 1½ hours until a skewer comes out clean. Remove from the oven and turn out on to a wire rack to cool. When cold, cut into pieces.

Wales

Cooking in Wales, especially in the outlying villages and farms, was always rather plain, and national dishes tended to be somewhat rural. The Methodists of the eighteenth century wiped out any luxury and indulgence, and ensured that plainness and severity were the order of the day. None the less, the traditional foods were healthy and filling. There was always a good supply of buttermilk, still used in cakes, breads and scones. Oats were widely grown on Welsh farms; oatmeal was a common ingredient in breads and cakes as well as being a thickening agent in stews and broths. In the days when cooking was done on an open range, cakes and scones were often baked on a griddle or bakestone that sat on the burning coals or wood. A makeshift oven could also be created by upturning the large iron cooking pot over the hot stone. But in most farmhouses a bread oven was built into the fireplace. This was heated with a wood fire and the ashes were raked out. The bread was put in first and the door sealed with clay for about two hours. Then the cakes and pastries were cooked and lastly a large rice pudding was left inside the cooling oven ready for the family meal in the evening.

Tea has always been a popular meal in Wales, not every day but on Sundays and special occasions. The favourite cakes are Welsh cakes, baked on a bakestone and traditionally offered to travellers as a snack between lunch and supper.

CHIRK CASTLE

Castell y Waun – Meadow Castle – is an apt name for a building in such a beautiful situation, with magnificent views over the wooded agricultural landscape of the Welsh borders. Started in around 1295 as part of Edward I's campaign to subdue the Welsh, Chirk's fortress-like exterior contrasts with the domestic interiors produced by the Myddelton family who have lived here since 1595.

In 1911 Chirk was leased to Lord Howard de Walden whose wife organised house parties between the wars. Guests included royalty and such famous people as George Bernard Shaw. When the family were alone at home they did not take tea (they always had a very substantial three- or four-course lunch at 1.30pm and a six-course dinner at 7.45pm, so perhaps it was not necessary), but when there were house guests afternoon tea took place in the salon, with beautiful bone china, a silver teapot and a hot-water jug with a silver methylated-spirit stove to keep the water hot.

Afternoon tea was never an elaborate meal, consisting of tiny sandwiches about the size of a postage stamp with the crusts removed. Sometimes in cold weather a dish of hot muffins or buttered scones was also served. According to the footman who was responsible for bringing in the tea: 'When clearing away the teas I always remember you had to eat at least four sandwiches to even taste them.'

Fruit Cheesecake

Makes 1 × 10in (25cm) round cake

FOR THE BASE
8oz (225g) digestive biscuits
4oz (100g) butter or margarine
1lb (450g) cream cheese, softened

3oz (75g) caster sugar
10fl oz (300ml) double or whipping
 cream

FOR THE TOPPING
6–7 fresh kiwi fruit, sliced,
 or 1lb (450g) fresh strawberries,
 sliced, or tinned black or red
 cherry fruit filling

Grease a 10in (25cm) loose-bottomed round flat tin. Crush the biscuits finely. Melt the butter or margarine and mix with the biscuit crumbs. Press into the prepared tin and smooth with a palette knife. Beat together the cream cheese and sugar until smooth and light. Whip the cream and mix into the cheese mixture. (In hot weather dissolve a teaspoon of gelatine into the mixture.) Spread over the biscuit base and leave to set. To serve, arrange the sliced fruit or tinned fruit filling over the top and serve immediately.

The topping may be varied according to which fruits are in season or according to taste.

Light Sponge Cake

Makes 1 × 8in (20cm) round cake

1 cup granulated or caster sugar
2 large or 3 medium eggs
1 cup self-raising flour, sifted
a pinch of salt

1 teaspoon baking powder
½ cup milk
2oz (50g) margarine or butter
2–3 drops vanilla essence

Preheat the oven to gas mark 3/325°F/160°C. Grease and line an 8in (20cm) round tin. Beat together the sugar and eggs until thick and creamy. Add the flour, salt and baking powder and mix well. Put the milk in a small pan and heat gently. Melt the butter or margarine in the milk and bring to the boil. When boiling, add to the flour mixture with the vanilla essence and beat well to give a runny consistency. Turn into the prepared tin and bang the tin sharply on the table to remove air bubbles. Bake for 20–25 minutes until a skewer comes out clean. Remove from the oven and cool in the tin for 15 minutes before turning out on to a wire rack to cool completely.

This cake is quick and easy to make, and is delicious served with fruit and cream. It is ideal for freezing.

ERDDIG

Visitors to Erddig are treated like servants. Instead of being welcomed at the front door, as if friends of the family, they are ushered through the estate yards. All great houses buried in the country were once the heart of a self-sufficient community, but Erddig presents a unique picture of how these empires were nurtured day by day. Judging by the staff portraits in the servants' hall, life was agreeable here: one of the house-maids is depicted at the age of eighty-seven.

It was weather damage which led Philip Yorke I to reface the west front of the house which his great-uncle, the successful London lawyer John Meller, had acquired in 1716. James Wyatt's rather bleak neo-classical composition contrasts with the warm brickwork of the garden front, where a pronounced change in the colour of the materials marks the wings added on either side of the late seventeenth-century block.

A visit by Queen Mary on 16 August 1921 was recorded in minute detail, from the moment the Queen arrived and toured the lower parts of the house, including the servants' hall, to afternoon tea in the dining-room. It seems that everybody was so busy chattering round the tea table that no one noticed the Queen's entry; as a result she sat at Mr Yorke's right hand rather than at the head of the table. But it didn't seem to matter. After tea cigarettes were handed round, and the Queen's ash dropped on to the carpet. Rubbing it in with her foot, she was heard to remark: 'I am told it is very good for the carpet.' The morning after the three-hour visit, a signed photograph from the Queen arrived by post with a letter from her secretary. Both the photograph and the letter are now on show in the saloon.

Bara Brith

Makes 1 × 2lb (900g) loaf

12oz (350g) mixed dried fruit
12fl oz (350ml) red wine
4oz (100g) margarine
4oz (100g) light soft brown sugar
2fl oz (50ml) milk

1 tablespoon black treacle
8oz (225g) self-raising flour, sifted
1 teaspoon mixed spice
2 eggs, beaten

Soak the fruit in the red wine overnight. The next day preheat the oven to gas mark 4/350°F/180°C. Grease and line a 2lb (900g) loaf tin. Add the margarine, sugar, milk and treacle to the fruit, bring to the boil and simmer for 5 minutes. Remove from the heat and leave to cool. Add the flour, mixed spice and beaten eggs and beat well with a wooden spoon. Turn into the prepared tin and bake just below the middle of the oven for 1–1¼ hours until a skewer comes out clean. Remove from the oven and leave to cool in the tin for 15 minutes before turning out on to a wire rack to cool completely. Serve sliced with butter.

Each region has its own version of this traditional Welsh tea bread. This one may be made with cold tea instead of red wine.

Economy Shortbread

1lb (450g) plain flour, sifted
7oz (200g) margarine, softened

4oz (100g) caster sugar

Preheat the oven to gas mark 5/375°F/190°C. Grease two 7in (17·5cm) round sandwich tins. Mix all the ingredients together to make a crumbly mixture and press into the prepared tins. Smooth the top with a palette knife, prick all over with a fork and bake for 20–25 minutes until pale golden. Remove from the oven and leave to cool in the tin. When cold, turn out and cut each round into portions.

Shortbread was first made by the Romans for their wedding rituals. It was the custom to break a wheaten cake over the head of the bride during the ceremony, so the cake had to be light and crumbly. The word 'short' means fat; the more fat a cake mixture contains the shorter it is.

Welsh Seed Cake

Makes 1 × 2lb (900g) loaf

8oz (225g) self-raising flour, sifted
1 teaspoon baking powder
6oz (175g) caster sugar
6oz (175g) margarine, softened

3 eggs, beaten
2–3fl oz (50–75ml) water
2–3 teaspoons caraway seeds

Preheat the oven to gas mark 5/375°F/190°C. Grease and line a 2lb (900g) loaf tin. Mix together the flour and baking powder. Add the sugar, margarine and eggs and beat well. Add enough of the water to give a soft, dropping consistency and beat hard for a minute or two. Add the caraway seeds and beat for a little longer. Turn into the prepared tin and bake just below the middle of the oven for 1¼ hours until a skewer comes out clean. Remove from the oven and leave to cool in the tin for about 10 minutes before turning out on to a wire rack to cool completely. Or you can add 2oz (50g) chopped walnuts instead of the caraway seeds.

PENRHYN CASTLE

Penrhyn is a late Georgian masterpiece, the outstanding product of a short-lived neo-Norman revival. Designed by Thomas Hopper, it was commissioned in 1820 by G. H. Dawkins Pennant to replace the neo-Gothic house by Samuel Wyatt he had inherited from his cousin. Whereas Richard Pennant had the benefit of a fortune made from Jamaican estates (as a result of which he strongly opposed the abolition of the slave trade), his cousin built lavishly on the profits of the Penrhyn slate quarries, exporting over 12,000 tons a year by 1792.

Penrhyn is uniquely all of a piece, built with slate as well as on its proceeds. In the oppressive Ebony Room, original green and red curtains and upholstery and faded red damask wall hangings give some relief from the black ebony furniture and the black surrounds to the fireplace and doorways. Huge plantain leaves on the firescreen recall the Jamaican estates. In the much lighter drawing-room next door, where afternoon tea was always served, mirrors at either end reflect two immense metalwork candelabra. Dotted around the house there are various pieces of tea ware, including a brass samovar, a copper teapot with its stand and lamp, a Regency rosewood teapoy, a silver-plated teapot and an early-morning tea set of Cauldon china which was bought from Mortlocks in Oxford Street.

Welsh Cheese and Herb Scones

Makes approximately 12 scones

1lb (450g) self-raising flour, sifted
1 teaspoon salt
4oz (100g) margarine, softened
1 teaspoon mixed dried herbs

8oz (225g) Cheddar or other strong cheese, grated
8 tablespoons milk
8 tablespoons water

Preheat the oven to gas mark 7/425°F/220°C. Grease a baking tray. Mix together the flour and salt and rub in the margarine. Add the herbs and 6oz (175g) of the cheese. Add the milk and water and mix to a soft dough. On a floured board, roll out to a thickness of 1in (2·5cm) and cut into rounds using a 2½in (6cm) cutter. Place on the prepared tray, top each scone with a little of the remaining grated cheese and bake for 10 minutes until golden. Remove from the oven and lift on to a wire rack to cool slightly. Serve warm or cold with butter.

POWIS CASTLE

Some time around 1200 the Welsh princes of Powis began building their new stronghold on this splendid defensive site, a great outcrop of limestone plunging steeply to the south with panoramic views over the River Severn to the hills of Shropshire. Although long since converted to a country house, Powis still has the trappings of a castle.

The front door opens into another world, with magnificent interiors fitted out for William Herbert, 3rd Lord Powis, 1st Earl, Marquis and titular Duke, a staunch supporter of the Stuart cause who spent his last years in exile with James II. The formal apartments contrast with the T-shaped long gallery, the only surviving Elizabethan interior dating from Sir Edward Herbert's acquisition of the castle in 1587. An ancient Roman sculpture of a more than life-size cat came to Powis through the marriage of the daughter of the house to the eldest son of Clive of India in 1784. In the Clive Museum Indian curiosities acquired by the Great Nabob and his son, who was Governor of Madras, are suggestive of great wealth and exoticism.

On 5 November 1839 Clive of India's great-grandson celebrated his twenty-first birthday, and there was much rejoicing in the nearby town of Welshpool. The day was proclaimed a general holiday, there was a 21-round salute of cannon fire, a procession with a band and, at eight o'clock in the evening, a huge firework display. On the Wednesday there was a tea party for the 'poor female inhabitants of the parish' provided by the Countess of Powis, and on the Thursday there was a stag hunt and a grand public dinner.

A Christmas Tea, clockwise from top: mincemeat cake (page 76); Grasmere gingerbread (page 122), Christmas cake (page 50); Ripon Christmas bread (page 108).

Welsh Cakes

Makes 10-12 cakes

8oz (225g) self-raising flour, sifted
a pinch of salt
2oz (50g) lard, softened
2oz (50g) margarine, softened
3oz (75g) granulated sugar

1oz (25g) currants
½ egg, beaten
1½ tablespoons milk
caster sugar for sprinkling

Preheat a griddle or a heavy frying pan to a moderate, even temperature. Mix together the flour and salt and rub in the fat. Add the sugar and currants and mix with the egg and milk to a soft dough. On a floured board, roll out to a thickness of ¼–½in (0·5–1cm) and cut out rounds using a 3in (7·5cm) cutter. Place on the griddle and cook both sides until light golden. Lift on to a wire rack to cool and sprinkle with caster sugar before serving.

Welsh cakes were traditionally cooked on a bakestone that sat on the open kitchen fire. Their name in Welsh is *pice ar y maen* which literally means 'cakes on the stone'.

Regional Specialities

Pembrokeshire Buns

Makes 11 buns

½oz (15g) lard, softened
½oz (15g) butter, softened
1lb (450g) plain flour, sifted
2oz (50g) caster sugar
2oz (50g) currants

1oz (25g) mixed candied peel
1oz (25g) fresh yeast
9fl oz (250ml) warm milk and
    water, mixed

Grease two baking trays. Rub the fat into the flour. Add the sugar, currants and peel and stir well. Dissolve the yeast in the milk and water and add to the dry ingredients. Mix to a soft dough and leave in a warm place to rise for 15 minutes. On a lightly floured board, knead the dough and then divide it into eleven 3oz (75g) pieces. Roll with the hands to form round buns, place on the prepared trays and leave in a warm place for 10 minutes until well risen. Meanwhile preheat the oven to gas mark 6/400°F/200°C. When the buns are well risen, bake for 15-20 minutes until golden. Remove from the oven and lift on to a wire rack to cool.

These buns used to be made for New Year celebrations in Pembrokeshire.

The housekeeper's dry stores cupboard at Wimpole Hall, Cambridgeshire.

Threshing Cake

Makes 1 × 2lb (900g) loaf

8oz (225g) plain flour, sifted
4oz (100g) dripping or lard
4oz (100g) caster sugar
8oz (225g) mixed dried fruit
1 egg, beaten

¼ teaspoon bicarbonate of soda
    dissolved in 1 tablespoon
    buttermilk or sour milk
a little extra buttermilk or sour milk

Preheat the oven to gas mark 5/375°F/190°C. Grease and line a 2lb (900g) loaf tin. Rub the fat into the flour. Add the sugar and dried fruit and stir well. Add the beaten egg and bicarbonate of soda and mix with enough buttermilk or sour milk to give a soft consistency. Turn into the prepared tin and bake for 1½ hours until a skewer comes out clean. Remove from the oven and turn on to a wire rack to cool.

Many areas of Britain had their own dishes for threshing time, and this fruit loaf was a Welsh speciality.

Welsh Honey Bread

Makes 1 × 1lb (450g) loaf

2oz (50g) butter, softened
1oz (25g) caster sugar
2 tablespoons clear honey
1 egg
2 tablespoons milk

8oz (225g) plain flour, sifted
1 teaspoon baking powder
¼ teaspoon salt
½ teaspoon mixed spice

Preheat the oven to gas mark 5/375°F/190°C. Grease a 1lb (450g) loaf tin. Beat together the butter, sugar and honey until light and fluffy. Whisk together the egg and milk and add to the mixture with the flour, baking powder, salt and spice. Mix to a soft dough. Turn into the prepared tin and bake for 40-45 minutes until firm and golden. Remove from the oven and turn out on to a wire rack to cool.

Welsh Honey and Ginger Cake

Makes 1 × 8in (20cm) round cake

4oz (100g) butter
8oz (225g) clear honey
5fl oz (150ml) milk
1lb (450g) plain flour, sifted
a pinch of salt

2½ teaspoons baking powder
3 teaspoons ground ginger
4oz (100g) sultanas
2oz (50g) mixed candied peel
2 eggs, beaten

Preheat the oven to gas mark 4/350°F/180°C. Grease and line an 8in (20cm) round tin. Melt the butter gently with the honey and milk. Remove from the heat and leave to cool. Mix together the flour, salt, baking powder, ginger and dried fruit. Add the beaten eggs and the butter mixture and mix to a soft consistency. Turn into the prepared tin and bake for 1¼-1½ hours until a skewer comes out clean. (Check the top after half an hour and, if it is beginning to brown too much, cover with a double layer of greaseproof paper.) Remove from the oven and turn out on to a wire rack to cool.

Welsh Lardy Cake

Makes 9 generous pieces

½ oz (15g) fresh yeast
1 tablespoon caster sugar
10fl oz (300ml) warm water
1lb (450g) plain flour, sifted
1 teaspoon salt
8oz (225g) lard, softened

4oz (100g) currants
2oz (50g) mixed candied peel
2oz (50g) caster or granulated
   sugar
a little extra plain flour

Cream together the yeast and caster sugar and mix with the warm water. Mix together the flour and salt, add the yeast mixture and mix to a soft dough. Knead for 3–4 minutes, then put in a bowl and leave in a warm place for 1–1½ hours until doubled in size. Preheat the oven to gas mark 6/400°F/200°C. Grease a 9in (22·5cm) square tin. On a floured board, roll out the dough to a thickness of ½in (1cm). Divide the lard, currants, peel and sugar into four equal portions. Spread a quarter of the lard on the dough and sprinkle over a quarter of the currants, peel and sugar and a little flour. Fold the dough in half and repeat the rolling, dotting and folding process three more times until all the ingredients are used. Place the folded dough in the prepared tin and bake for 25–30 minutes until golden brown. Remove from the oven and leave to cool in the tin. When cold, cut into squares and lift out of the tin. To serve, warm in the oven or microwave.

Lardy cake was made to use up some of the fat left over from the family pig after the annual slaughter. Until early in the twentieth century, most rural families kept at least one pig, fattening it up on all the waste food during the year and then killing it in the autumn to provide food through the winter. Nothing was wasted: bacon, ham, fresh and salt pork provided joints of meat as well as meat for stews and hot pots; trotters were used for brawn; the head was boiled to make a strong jelly stock; the cheeks were made into 'Bath chaps'; the offal went into black puddings; scraps made pork pies; dripping was spread on bread and toast; and the lard was used for frying and for making pastry, puddings and lardy cakes.

Northern Ireland

Much of Irish traditional cookery among the wealthy classes was similar to that of England or Scotland, but often with local variations. Working people relied heavily on the potato and on a good supply of milk, buttermilk and cream in order merely to survive. Many traditional Irish dishes using potatoes have acquired unusual names: dippity is a mixture of raw, grated potatoes, flour, milk, eggs and salt cooked as little round cakes; champ is made with mashed potatoes, spring onions, milk and butter and is eaten with melted butter poured over the top; and boxty, a Hallowe'en speciality, is cooked as pancakes, dumplings or bread.

Cakes and breads tended to be rather plain, but were often made more interesting by the addition of apples and dried fruit. As with early baking in other parts of Britain, caraway seeds and currants made everyday dough into festive cakes and breads, lightening the monotony of simple fare. A special ingredient was Irish whiskey, which was sometimes added to fruit cakes and seed cakes. The desire for sweetmeats was also satisfied by farls, round cakes divided into four equal parts (farls) and spread with butter and homemade jams, or barm brack, Ireland's traditional fruited tea bread. 'Barm' means leaven or yeast; 'brack' refers to the little dots that are the fruit in the cake. At Hallowe'en a silver sixpenny is wrapped and hidden inside the loaf and is supposed to bring good luck to whomever finds it in their serving.

A favourite meal in Ireland was high tea, which originated during the Industrial Revolution of the nineteenth century when workers needed a hearty meal on their return home after a long, hard day in the factories, mines and workshops. In contrast with afternoon tea (also known as low tea), high tea is taken at the dining table and usually consists of savoury dishes, such as pies, cold meats or cheese on toast, followed by home-baked bread with cheese and jam, fruit loaves and cakes of all descriptions. It has not changed significantly since Victorian days and is still popular in the north of England, in Scotland and amongst families with children who appreciate a filling meal when school is over for the day.

CASTLE WARD

Castle Ward is a bizarre house situated high up on the southern tip of Strangford Lough in County Down. Although built at one period, from 1762-70, it is classical on the east side and Gothick on the west. This architectural curiosity is a result of the opposing tastes of Bernard Ward, later 1st Viscount Bangor, and his wife Lady Anne. Although the stylistic division of Castle Ward was followed by the separation of Bernard and Anne, and by her departure for Bath, the elaborate decorative schemes have survived almost unaltered.

The wife of the 6th Viscount Bangor made a habit of serving afternoon tea in her sitting-room if the number of guests was small. She used a willow-pattern tea service, derived in England from a Chinese version of an English idea of a Chinese scene. The Staffordshire potteries printed the majority of their products with blue decoration, often in the Chinese style. The willow pattern is believed to have originated in 1780 and Thomas Minton is often credited with having engraved the first. Before setting up his own pottery in the 1790s, Minton worked as a master graver in London and supplied Josiah Spode with designs. It is thought that the first willow pattern was made for the Spode factory.

Boiled Whiskey Cake

Makes 1 × 2lb (900g) loaf

10oz (275g) raisins and currants
8fl oz (225ml) water
8oz (225g) light or dark soft brown sugar
4oz (100g) margarine
8oz (225g) plain flour, sifted

2 teaspoons mixed spice
1½ teaspoons bicarbonate of soda
1½ teaspoons ground ginger
2 large eggs, beaten
2fl oz (50ml) Irish whiskey

Preheat the oven to gas mark 3/325°F/160°C. Grease and line a 2lb (900g) loaf tin. Put the mixed fruit, water, sugar and margarine into a pan and bring to the boil, stirring occasionally. Leave to cool for a few minutes. Add a little of the flour, the mixed spice, bicarbonate of soda and ginger, then mix and leave to stand until cool. Add the beaten eggs, the whiskey and the remaining flour, mix well and turn into the prepared tin. Bake for 1½-1¾ hours until a skewer comes out clean. Remove from the oven and turn out on to a wire rack to cool.

Gypsy Creams

Makes 24 double biscuits

FOR THE BISCUITS
6oz (175g) margarine, softened
2oz (50g) white shortening
  (Trex or similar)
6oz (175g) caster sugar
2 teaspoons golden syrup

8oz (225g) plain wholemeal flour,
  sifted
1 teaspoon baking powder
1 teaspoon bicarbonate of soda

FOR THE FILLING
4oz (100g) margarine or butter,
  softened
2oz (50g) cream cheese

4oz (100g) icing sugar, sifted
2oz (50g) cocoa powder, sifted

Preheat the oven to gas mark 2/300°F/150°C. Grease two or three baking trays. Beat together the margarine, white shortening and sugar until light and fluffy. Add the syrup and beat again. Add the flour, baking powder and bicarbonate of soda and mix thoroughly. On a lightly floured board, roll out and cut into rounds using a 2in (5cm) cutter. Place on the prepared trays, leaving plenty of room for the biscuits to spread, and bake for 10 minutes until firm and golden. Remove from the oven and lift on to a wire rack to cool. To make the filling, beat all the ingredients until light and fluffy and use to sandwich the biscuits together.

What a part of confidante has that poor teapot played ever since the kindly plant was introduced among us. What myriads of women have cried over it, to be sure! What sickbeds it has smoked by! What fevered lips have received refreshment from it! Nature meant very kindly by women when she made the tea plant; and with a little thought, what a series of pictures and groups the fancy may conjure up and assemble round the teapot and cup.

William Makepeace Thackeray (1811-63), *Pendennis*

Sweetmince Squares

Makes 15 squares

1½ lb (675g) rich shortcrust pastry (see page 16)
1½ teaspoons cornflour
½ teaspoon custard powder
6fl oz (175ml) water
6oz (175g) currants and raisins
2oz (50g) mixed candied peel

3oz (75g) caster, granulated or demerara sugar
1 teaspoon ground cinnamon
1 teaspoon mixed spice
½ teaspoon ground ginger
caster sugar for dredging

Make the pastry according to the instructions on page 16 and chill for at least 15 minutes. Preheat the oven to gas mark 4/350°F/180°C. Grease a 7 × 11in (17·5 × 27·5cm) Swiss roll tin. On a floured board, roll out half the pastry and use to line the prepared tin. Mix together the cornflour and custard powder with the water and put with all the other ingredients for the filling into a pan. Bring to the boil and simmer until thick. Turn into the pastry case and spread evenly. Roll out the remaining pastry and lay on top. Wet the edges of the pastry with a little water or milk and press well together. Bake for 45–50 minutes until golden. Remove from the oven and dredge with caster sugar. Allow to cool in the tin. When cold, cut into squares.

FLORENCE COURT

Florence Court in County Fermanagh is one of the most important examples of eighteenth-century Irish architecture and interior rococo plasterwork decoration. It was built in about 1750 by John Cole, father of the 1st Earl of Enniskillen, and the house's charm and eccentricity are matched by the beauty of the mountains and wild countryside that surround it. The 3rd Earl was a world-famous collector of fossils whose collection contained some 10,000 specimens. It became one of the most important private collections anywhere in the world and remained at Florence Court for fifty years, until the Earl transferred it to the British Museum in London. During his time at Florence Court he entertained many eminent geologists and scientists, including Sir Charles Owen, the inventor of the word 'dinosaur'.

Florence Court is quite close to the Belleek pottery, and a distinctive chamber pot with a picture of Gladstone in the bottom bears witness to this. The pot dates back to the political situation in the late nineteenth century, when Gladstone advocated home rule for Ireland but could not carry it in Parliament; chamber pots decorated with his face were manu-factured as an insult to him.

Pineapple Boiled Cake

Makes 1 × 2lb (900g) loaf

8oz (225g) tinned crushed pineapple with its juice
2oz (50g) margarine
2oz (50g) light or dark soft brown sugar
6oz (175g) mixed dried fruit
2 large eggs, beaten
2oz (50g) glacé cherries, cut into quarters
4oz (100g) self-raising flour, sifted
a pinch of salt
½ teaspoon mixed spice
½ teaspoon bicarbonate of soda

Preheat the oven to gas mark 4/350°F/180°C. Grease and line a 2lb (900g) loaf tin. Put the pineapple, margarine, sugar, dried fruit and cherries into a saucepan, bring to the boil and boil for about 6 minutes. Leave to cool. When cold, add the flour, salt, mixed spice, bicarbonate of soda and beaten eggs and mix thoroughly. Turn into the prepared tin and bake for 40–45 minutes until a skewer comes out clean. Remove from the oven and turn out on to a wire rack to cool.

GIANT'S CAUSEWAY

The Giant's Causeway on the north Antrim coast has been a mecca for tourists since the eighteenth century. In the tertiary era, 60 million years ago, lava poured out through fissures in the earth's surface to flow over the chalk and solidify into basalt, much of it polygonal in section. Most of the columns are six-sided, but some have four, five, seven or ten sides.

If the causeway itself is fascinating, the coast to which it leads is truly spectacular. The Trust has acquired the land, or rights of way, to make a twelve-mile walk along, above and below the cliffs. The path passes the romantic ruins of Dunseverick Castle, the oldest and once the most strongly fortified place in Ireland, and ends at the rock island of Carrick-a-Rede, 'the rock on the road', the road being the path of the salmon on their way to the Rivers Bann and Bush. During the fishing season the sixty-foot chasm between the island and the cliff is spanned by a rope bridge. The salmon do not swim through the narrows below it, but go north round the island where the fishermen have set their nets for centuries.

John Keats spoke of lovers who
'nibble their toast, and cool their tea with sighs'.

Almond Slices

Makes 12 slices

FOR THE PASTRY
8oz (225g) plain flour, sifted
4oz (100g) margarine, softened
2oz (50g) caster sugar

1 egg, beaten
a little cold water, if needed

FOR THE TOPPING
8-9oz (225-250g) strawberry jam
4oz (100g) caster sugar
4oz (100g) icing sugar, sifted
4oz (100g) ground almonds
2oz (50g) semolina

1 whole egg and 1 egg white, beaten
   together
a few drops of almond essence
2oz (50g) blanched split almonds
   to decorate

Make the pastry by rubbing the margarine into the flour until the mixture resembles breadcrumbs. Add the sugar and bind together with the egg and enough water to give a soft, pliable dough. Place in a plastic bag and chill for at least 15 minutes. Preheat the oven to gas mark 6/400°F/200°C. Grease a 7 × 11in (17·5 × 27·5cm) Swiss roll tin. On a lightly floured board, roll out the pastry and use to line the base of the prepared tin. (If the pastry is quite wet and too soft to roll, press into the tin with floured fingers.) Spread the strawberry jam over the base. Place all the dry ingredients for the topping in a bowl. Add the beaten egg and almond essence and mix carefully until the mixture binds together. Spread over the jam, sprinkle with split almonds and bake for 20-30 minutes until golden and well risen. Remove from oven and leave to cool in tin. When cold, cut into slices and lift carefully from the tin.

Giant's Boiled Fruit Cake

Makes 1 × 2lb (900g) loaf

6oz (175g) butter, softened
6oz (175g) granulated or caster
   sugar
10fl oz (300ml) water
4oz (100g) raisins
4oz (100g) sultanas
4oz (100g) currants

2oz (50g) glacé cherries, halved
8oz (225g) plain flour, sifted
2 teaspoons mixed spice
1 teaspoon baking powder
1 teaspoon ground ginger
2oz (50g) walnuts, roughly chopped
2 large eggs, beaten

Put the butter, sugar, water, dried fruit and glacé cherries into a pan. Bring to the boil and simmer for 10 minutes. Remove from the heat and leave to stand overnight. The next day preheat the oven to gas mark 4/350°F/180°C. Grease and line a 2lb (900g) loaf tin. Mix together the dry ingredients and walnuts and add to the boiled mixture with the beaten eggs. Mix thoroughly and turn into the prepared tin. Bake for 1-1½ hours until a skewer comes out clean. Remove from the oven and leave to cool in the tin for about 15 minutes before turning out on to a wire rack to cool completely.

ROWALLANE GARDEN

The drumlin landscape of County Down is harsh farming country, where little fields formed on the thin soil are edged by dry-stone walls built from material laboriously cleared by hand. Features which would defeat most cultivators are the very essence of Rowallane. Established on the fields of a hill farm, the informal planting follows the lie of the land, banks of shrubs turning back on themselves round a hillock and natural rock gardens formed on craggy basalt outcrops.

Although started by the Reverend John Moore in the late nineteenth century, this unique tree and shrub garden is largely the creation of his talented nephew who inherited the property in 1903. Hugh Armytage Moore's genius lay in his ability to choose a plant for a setting, enhancing the natural landscape rather than adapting it to his own designs. The garden is particularly known for its spectacular displays of rhododendrons and azaleas; and many rare and exotic species, some sent back by E. H. Wilson, G. Forrest, F. Kingdon-Ward and other collectors from the Far East and the southern hemisphere, include the Chilean fire bush, the handkerchief tree and magnificent southern beeches. This is a garden where the beauty and subtle variety of foliage can be fully appreciated, every hue and tone of green seeming to contribute to the whole.

Banana and Fruit Cake

Makes 1 × 2lb (900g) loaf

3oz (75g) margarine, softened
4oz (100g) light or dark soft brown sugar
3 tablespoons clear honey
2 eggs, beaten
2 ripe bananas, mashed

8oz (225g) self-raising flour
1 teaspoon allspice
¼ teaspoon bicarbonate of soda
¼ teaspoon salt
8oz (225g) raisins

Preheat the oven to gas mark 4/350°F/180°C. Grease and line a 2lb (900g) loaf tin. Beat together the margarine and sugar until light and fluffy. Add the honey, eggs and bananas and beat well. Mix together the flour, allspice, bicarbonate of soda, salt and raisins and fold into the banana mixture. Mix well and then turn into the prepared tin. Bake for 1–1¼ hours until a skewer comes out clean. Remove from the oven and turn out on to a wire rack to cool.

Irish Plum Cake

Makes 1 × 8in (20cm) round cake

6oz (175g) butter, softened
6oz (175g) light or dark soft brown
   sugar
8oz (225g) plain flour, sifted
½ teaspoon mixed spice
1 teaspoon grated nutmeg
¼ teaspoon salt
the grated rind of half a lemon and
   half an orange
3 eggs, beaten
8oz (225g) sultanas

8oz (225g) raisins
4oz (100g) currants
2oz (50g) glacé cherries, halved
3oz (75g) mixed candied peel
2oz (50g) ready-to-use dried
   apricots
2oz (50g) ground almonds
2oz (50g) almonds, blanched and
   roughly chopped
2 tablespoons brandy, rum or Irish
   whiskey

Preheat the oven to gas mark 3/325°F/160°C. Grease and line an 8in (20cm) round tin. Beat together the butter and sugar until light and fluffy. Mix together the flour, spices, salt and lemon and orange rind. Add to the butter mixture a little at a time with the beaten eggs, beating well after each addition. Add the dried fruit and nuts with the alcohol and mix thoroughly so that all the ingredients are evenly distributed. Turn into the prepared tin and lightly hollow out the centre. Bake for 1½ hours until a skewer comes out clean. Remove from the oven and leave to cool in the tin for at least 15 minutes before turning out on to a wire rack to cool completely.

This rich fruit mixture is suitable as a Christmas or wedding cake. It differs from traditional English recipes by the addition of apricots.

Pratie Cake

Makes 1 × 7in (17·5cm) round cake

1lb (450g) potatoes, boiled and
   mashed
1 teaspoon salt
2oz (50g) butter or margarine,
   melted
4 tablespoons plain flour, sifted
4–6 cooking apples, peeled, cored
   and sliced

2 tablespoons demerara or light soft
   brown sugar
a little milk
1–2oz (25–50g) butter
demerara or caster sugar for
   dredging

Preheat the oven to gas mark 5/375°F/190°C. Grease a baking tray. Mix together the mashed potatoes, salt and butter or margarine and work in the flour to give a pliable dough. Knead lightly, then divide into two portions. On a floured board, roll each piece out into a round approximately 7in (17·5cm) in diameter, making one slightly larger than the other. Place the larger round on the baking tray and lay the apple slices on top of the dough. Sprinkle with the sugar. Dampen the edges of the dough with a little milk and lay the other round on top. Press the edges well together. Bake for 45–60 minutes until the apples are tender and the top is golden. Remove from the oven, spread with butter, dredge all over with sugar and serve hot.

If liked, add half a teaspoon of ground ginger to the mixture with the flour, and, if you prefer a sweeter cake, also add a little caster sugar.

Sweet Wholemeal Bannock

Makes 1 × 2lb (900g) loaf or 1 × 8in (20cm) round bannock

12oz (350g) plain wholemeal flour, sifted
4oz (100g) plain white flour, sifted
1 teaspoon bicarbonate of soda
2oz (50g) margarine, softened
2 dessertspoons caster sugar
7fl oz (200ml) buttermilk

Preheat the oven to gas mark 4/350°F/180°C. Grease and line a 2lb (900g) loaf tin or an 8in (20cm) round tin. Mix together the flours and bicarbonate of soda and rub in the margarine. Add the sugar and mix with the buttermilk to give a soft, pliable dough. Knead lightly, then shape to fit the tin. Place in the tin and bake for 35–45 minutes until well risen and golden. Remove from the oven and turn out on to a wire rack to cool. Serve warm, sliced with butter.

Regional Specialities

Barm Brack

Makes 1 × 2lb (900g) loaf

4oz (100g) currants
4oz (100g) sultanas
4oz (100g) raisins
2oz (50g) mixed candied peel
2oz (50g) glacé cherries, quartered
7oz (200g) light soft brown sugar
10fl oz (300ml) cold black tea
the grated rind of 1 lemon
2 eggs, beaten
9oz (250g) self-raising flour, sifted
1 teaspoon mixed spice
a pinch of salt

Put the dried fruit and glacé cherries into a bowl with the sugar, tea and lemon rind and leave to soak for at least 3 hours, preferably longer. Preheat the oven to gas mark 4/350°F/180°C. Grease and line a 2lb (900g) loaf tin. Add the eggs, flour, mixed spice and salt to the fruit mixture and mix thoroughly. Turn into the prepared tin and bake for 1½–1¾ hours until a skewer comes out clean. Remove from the oven and turn out on to a wire rack to cool. Serve sliced with butter.

Boxty Bread

Makes 2 small round flat loaves

8oz (225g) raw potatoes
8oz (225g) mashed potatoes
8oz (225g) plain flour, sifted

2oz (50g) butter, melted
salt and freshly ground black pepper

Preheat the oven to gas mark 5/375°F/190°C. Grease a baking tray. Wash and peel the raw potatoes. Grate into a clean cloth and wring well over a bowl to squeeze out the juice. Place the grated potatoes in a bowl with the mashed potatoes and mix well together. Leave the starchy liquid in the bowl until the starch has settled, then pour off the liquid and add the starch to the potatoes. Add the flour, melted butter and seasoning and mix to a soft dough. Knead well. Divide into two portions and, on a floured board, roll into flat rounds. Place on the baking tray and divide the top of each loaf into four with a sharp knife. Bake for 40 minutes until firm and golden. Remove from the oven and serve hot with plenty of butter.

Buttermilk Oaten Bread

Makes 2 small loaves

7oz (200g) fine oatmeal
10fl oz (300ml) buttermilk or sour milk

9oz (250g) plain flour, sifted
1 teaspoon baking powder
¼ teaspoon salt

Soak the oatmeal in the milk overnight. The following day preheat the oven to gas mark 4/350°F/180°C. Grease a baking tray. Mix together the flour, baking powder and salt. Add the oatmeal and milk mixture and mix well (if necessary adding a little more milk) to give a soft dough. Knead until smooth. Divide into two portions and, on a floured board, roll each portion out to a thickness of about 1in (2·5cm) and about 4in (10cm) in diameter. Place both loaves on the prepared tray and bake for 35–40 minutes until they are golden and sound hollow when tapped. Remove from the oven and serve hot with butter.

This is an easy and quick bread to make; it has a soft, moist texture and a lovely, nutty flavour.

Thank God for tea! What would the world do without tea?
How did it exist? I am glad I was not born before tea.

Sidney Smith (1771-1845), the evangelistic campaigner of his day

---

Irish Honey Scones

Makes 1 × 7in (17·5cm) round

4oz (100g) plain wholemeal flour, sifted
4oz (100g) plain white flour, sifted
2 teaspoons baking powder
a pinch of salt

3oz (75g) butter, softened
1 tablespoon light soft brown sugar
2 tablespoons clear honey
2–3fl oz (50–75ml) milk

Preheat the oven to gas mark 6/400°F/200°C. Grease a baking tray. Mix together the flour, baking powder and salt and rub in the butter. Add the sugar and mix. Mix the honey with the milk and stir until the honey has dissolved. Reserve a little for glazing and add the rest to the flour. Mix to a soft dough. Place the dough on the prepared tray and shape with the hands into a flat round approximately 7in (17·5cm) in diameter. Divide the top into eight wedges. Bake for 15–20 minutes. Remove from the oven, glaze the top with the honey and milk mixture and return to the oven for a further 5–10 minutes until golden. Remove from the oven and serve warm with butter.

Irish Potato Cakes

Makes 6 cakes

4oz (100g) cold mashed potatoes
4oz (100g) plain white flour, sifted
2oz (50g) lard or dripping

a pinch of salt
a little milk

Preheat the oven to gas mark 6/400°F/200°C. Grease a baking tray. Mix together the potatoes and flour and rub in the fat. Add the salt and enough milk to give a soft, pliable dough. Roll out on a floured board to a thickness of ½in (1cm) and cut into rounds using a 2½in (6cm) cutter. Place on the prepared tray and bake for 15–20 minutes until golden. Remove from the oven and serve piping hot, spread with butter.

These traditional savoury cakes are excellent served for breakfast, tea or supper.

National Trust Restaurants and Tea-rooms

BERKSHIRE

Basildon Park
License applied for restaurant
Lower Basildon, Reading
RG8 9NR
Tel: (0118) 984 4080

Cliveden
Licensed restaurant
The Conservatory Restaurant,
Taplow, Maidenhead
SL6 0JA
Tel: (01628) 661406

BUCKINGHAMSHIRE

Claydon House
Unlicensed tea-room
Middle Claydon,
near Buckingham
MK18 2EY
Tel: (01296) 730954

Hughenden Manor
Licensed restaurant
High Wycombe HP14 4LA
Tel: (01494) 755576

Stowe Gardens
Licensed restaurant
Buckingham MK18 5EH
Tel: (01280) 815819

Waddesdon Manor
Licensed restaurant
Waddesdon, near Aylesbury
HP18 0JH
Tel: (01296) 651211/282

CAMBRIDGESHIRE

Anglesey Abbey
Licensed restaurant
Lode, Cambridge CB5 9EJ
Tel: (01223) 811175

Houghton Mill
Unlicensed restaurant
Houghton,
near Huntingdon
PE17 2AZ
Tel: (01480) 462413

Peckover House
Licensed tea-room
North Brink, Wisbech
PE13 1JR
Tel: (01945) 583463

Wicken Fen
Unlicensed kiosk
Lode Lane,
Wicken, Ely
CB7 5XP
Tel: (01353) 720274

Wimpole Hall
Licensed restaurant
The Old Rectory Restaurant,
Arrington, near Royston
SG8 0BW
Tel: (01223) 208670

Wimpole Home Farm
Unlicensed café
Arrington, near Royston
SG8 0BW
Tel: (01223) 208987

CHESHIRE

Dunham Massey
Licensed restaurant
The Stables Restaurant,
near Altrincham
WA14 4SJ
Tel: (0161) 941 2815

Little Moreton Hall
Licensed tea-room
near Congleton
CW12 4SD
Tel: (01260) 272 018

Lyme Park
Licensed tea-room
Disley, Stockport
SK12 2NX
Tel: (01663) 762023

CORNWALL

Carnewas
near Bedruthan Steps
Unlicensed tea-room
Carnewas Tea-room,
St Eval, Wadebridge
PL27 7UW
Tel: (01637) 860701

Cotehele
Licensed restaurant
St Dominick, Saltash
PL12 6TA
Tel: (01579) 352711

Licensed tea-room
The Edgcumbe Arms,
The Quay, Cotehele,
St Dominick, Saltash
PL12 6TA
Tel: (01579) 350024

Lanhydrock
Licensed restaurant
Bodmin
PL30 5AD
Tel: (01208) 74331

St Michael's Mount
Licensed restaurant
The Sail Loft Restaurant,
Marazion
TR17 0HT
Tel: (01736) 710748

Trelissick Garden
Licensed restaurant
Feock, Truro
TR3 6QL
Tel: (01872) 863486

Trerice
Licensed tea-room
Kestle Mill, Newquay
TR8 4PG
Tel: (01673) 879434

CUMBRIA

Acorn Bank
Licensed tea-room
Temple Sowerby,
near Penrith
CA10 1SP
Tel: (017683) 61893

Fell Foot Park
Licensed tea-room
Newby Bridge,
Ulverston
LA12 8NN
Tel: (015395) 31273

Sizergh Castle
Licensed tea-room
near Kendal
LA8 8AE
Tel: (015395) 60070

Wordsworth House
Licensed tea-room
Main Street,
Cockermouth
CA13 9RX
Tel: (01900) 824820

DERBYSHIRE

Calke Abbey
Licensed restaurant
The Threshing Barn Restaurant,
Ticknall DE73 1LE
Tel: (01332) 86480

Hardwick Hall
Licensed restaurant
The Great Kitchen Restaurant,
Doe Lea,
Chesterfield
S44 5QJ
Tel: (01246) 854088

Ilam Hall
Unlicensed tea-room
The Manifold Tea-room,
Ilam, Ashbourne DE6 2AZ
Tel: (01335) 350245

Kedleston Hall
Licensed restaurant
Derby DE22 5JH
Tel: (01332) 842191

Longshaw
Unlicensed tea-room
Longshaw Information Centre,
Sheffield S11 7TZ
Tel: (01433) 631708

Sudbury Hall
Licensed tea-room
The Coach House Tea-room,
Sudbury DE6 5HT
Tel: (01283) 585337

DEVON

Arlington Court
Licensed restaurant
near Barnstaple
EX31 4LP
Tel: (01271) 850629

Buckland Abbey
Licensed restaurant
Yelverton, Plymouth PL20 6EY
Tel: (01822) 855024

Castle Drogo
Licensed restaurant
Drewsteignton EX6 6PB
Tel: (01647) 432629

Finch Foundry
Unlicensed tea-room
Sticklepath, Okehampton
EX20 2NW
Tel: (01837) 840046

Killerton
Licensed self-service restaurant
Broadclyst EX5 3LE
Tel: (01392) 881345

Knightshayes Court
Licensed self-service restaurant
Bolham, Tiverton
EX16 7RQ
Tel: (01884) 259416

Lydford Gorge
Unlicensed tea-room
The Stables, Lydford,
Okehampton
EX20 4BH
Tel: (01822) 820441

Overbecks
Unlicensed tea-room
Sharpitor, Salcombe
TQ8 8LW
Tel: (01548) 842893

Saltram House
Licensed restaurant
Plympton, Plymouth
PL7 1UH
Tel: (01752) 340635

Watersmeet House
Unlicensed tea-room
Watersmeet Rd, Lynmouth
EX35 6NT
Tel: (01598) 753348

DORSET

Brownsea Island
Unlicensed restaurant
Café Villano, Poole Harbour
BH15 7EE
Tel: (01202) 700244

Corfe Castle
Licensed tea-room
The Castle Tea-room,
The Square, near Wareham
BH20 5EZ
Tel: (01929) 481332

Kingston Lacy
Licensed restaurant
Wimborne Minster
BH21 4EA
Tel: (01202) 889242

Studland
Unlicensed tea-room
Knoll Beach Café, Knoll Beach
BH19 3AX
Tel: (01929) 450305

EAST SUSSEX

Bateman's
Licensed restaurant
Burwash, Etchingham
TN19 7DS
Tel: (01435) 882302

Bodiam Castle
Unlicensed tea-room
Wharfside Tea-room,
near Robertsbridge TN32 5UA
Tel: (01580) 830074

ESSEX

Flatford: Bridge Cottage
Licensed tea-room
Flatford, East Bergholt,
Colchester CO7 6OL
Tel: (01206) 298260

Hatfield Forest
Unlicensed tea-room
Lakeside Café, Takeley,
Bishop's Stortford CM22 6NE
Tel: (01279) 870579

GATESHEAD

Gibside
Unlicensed tea-room
near Rowlands Gill, Burnopfield,
Newcastle upon Tyne NE16 6BG
Tel: (01207) 545801

GLOUCESTERSHIRE

Dyrham Park
Licensed restaurant
Chippenham SN14 8ER
Tel: (0117) 9374293

Hidcote Manor Garden
*Licensed restaurant and
unlicensed tea-room*
The Garden Restaurant,
Hidcote Bartrim,
near Chipping Campden
GL55 6LR
Tel: (01386) 438703

HAMPSHIRE

Mottisfont Abbey
Licensed restaurant
Mottisfont, near Romsey
SO51 0LP
Tel: (01794) 340757

The Vyne
Licensed restaurant
The Brewhouse Restaurant,
Sherborne St John,
Basingstoke
RG24 9HL
Tel: (01256) 880039

HERTFORDSHIRE

Ashridge Estate
Unlicensed kiosk
The National Trust Visitor Centre,
Ringshall, Berkhamsted HP4 1LT
Tel: (01442) 851227

ISLE OF WIGHT

The Needles Old Battery
Unlicensed tea-room
West Highdown, Totland
PO39 0JH
Tel: (01983) 754772

KENT

Chartwell
Licensed restaurant
Westerham
TN16 1PS
Tel: (01732) 863087

Emmetts Garden
Licensed restaurant
Ide Hill, Sevenoaks
TN14 6AY
Tel: (01732) 863087

Ightham Mote
Unlicensed tea-room
Ivy Hatch, Sevenoaks
TN15 0NT
Tel: (01732) 811314

Knole
Unlicensed tea-room
Brewhouse Tea-room,
Sevenoaks
TN15 0RP
Tel: (01732) 741762

The White Cliffs of Dover
Unlicensed tea-room
Langdon Cliffs,
near Dover
CT16 1HJ
Tel: (01304) 242827

Sissinghurst Castle Garden
Licensed restaurant
The Granary Restaurant,
Sissinghurst,
near Cranbrook
TN17 2AB
Tel: (01580) 713097

LANCASHIRE

Rufford Old Hall
Licensed tea-room
Rufford, near Ormskirk
L40 1SG
Tel: (01704) 821254

LINCOLNSHIRE

Belton House
Licensed restaurant
The Stables Restaurant,
Belton, Grantham
NG32 2LS
Tel: (01476) 573086

LIVERPOOL

Speke Hall
Licensed (wine only) tea-room
The Walk L24 1XD
Tel: (0151) 427 7231

LONDON

Osterley Park
Licensed restaurant
Isleworth TW7 4RB
Tel: (020) 8569 7624

Sutton House
Licensed café/bar
2 & 4 Homerton High Street,
Hackney E9 6JQ
Tel: (020) 8525 9052

MIDDLESBROUGH

Ormesby Hall
Unlicensed tea-room
Middlesbrough
TS7 9AS
Tel: (01642) 324188

NORFOLK

Blickling Hall
Licensed restaurant
Blickling, Norwich
NR11 6NF
Tel: (01263) 738046

Felbrigg Hall
Licensed restaurant
The Park Restaurant,
Felbrigg NR11 8PR
Tel: (01263) 838237

Horsey Windpump
Unlicensed kiosk
Horsey Staithe Stores,
Horsey,
Great Yarmouth
NR29 4EF
Tel: (01493) 393904

Oxburgh Hall
Licensed restaurant
Oxborough, King's Lynn
PE33 9PS
Tel: (01366) 328243

NORTHAMPTONSHIRE

Canons Ashby House
Unlicensed tea-room
The Brewhouse Tea-room,
Canons Ashby, Daventry
NN11 3SD
Tel: (01327) 860044

NORTHERN IRELAND

The Argory
Unlicensed tea-room
Moy, Dungannon,
Co. Tyrone BT71 6NA
Tel: (028) 8778 4753

Crom Estate
Unlicensed tea-room
Newtownbutler,
Co. Fermanagh
BT92 8AP
Tel: (028) 6773 8118

Castle Ward
Unlicensed restaurant
Strangford, Downpatrick,
Co. Down BT30 7LS
Tel: (028) 4488 1204

Giant's Causeway
Unlicensed restaurant
The Giant's Pantry
44a Causeway Road,
Bushmills, Co. Antrim
BT57 8SU
Tel: (028) 2073 2282

Mount Stewart
Unlicensed tea-room
The Ark Club Tea Room,
Portaferry Road, Newtownards,
Co. Down BT22 2AD
Tel: (028) 4278 8801

Springhill
Unlicensed tea-room
20 Springhill Rd,
Moneymore,
Magherafelt,
Co. Londonderry
BT45 7NQ
Tel: (028) 8674 8210

Wellbrook Beetling Mill
Unlicensed tea-room
20 Wellbrook Rd,
Cookstown,
Corkhill,
Co. Tyrone
BT80 9RY
Tel: (028) 8675 1715

NORTHUMBERLAND

Cragside
Licensed restaurant
The Vickers Rooms Restaurant,
Rothbury, Morpeth
NE65 7PX
Tel: (01669) 620134

**Hadrian's Wall
& Housesteads Fort**
Unlicensed refreshments kiosk
Bardon Mill,
Hexham
NE47 6NN
Tel: (01434) 344525

Wallington
Unlicensed tea-room
The Clock Tower Tea Room,
Cambo,
Morpeth
NE61 4AR
Tel: (01670) 774274

NOTTINGHAMSHIRE

Clumber Park
Licensed restaurant and tea-room
Worksop
S80 3AZ
Tel: (01909) 484122

OXFORDSHIRE

Greys Court
Unlicensed tea-room
Rotherfield Greys,
Henley-on-Thames RG9 4PG
Tel: (01491) 628529

Upton House
Unlicensed tea-room
Banbury OX15 6HT
Tel: (01295) 670266

SHROPSHIRE

Attingham Park
Licensed tea-room
Shrewsbury SY4 4TP
Tel: (01743) 709203

Carding Mill Valley
Unlicensed café
Chalet Pavilion,
Church Stretton
SY6 6JG
Tel: (01694) 722631

Dudmaston
Unlicensed tea-room
Quatt, Bridgnorth WV15 6QN
Tel: (01746) 780866

SOMERSET

Barrington Court
Licensed restaurant
near Ilminster
TA19 0NQ
Tel: (01460) 241244

Montacute House
Licensed restaurant
Montacute TA15 6XP
Tel: (01935) 826294

Tintinhull
Unlicensed tea-room
Stable Tea-Rooms,
Farm Street, Yeovil BA22 9PZ
Tel: (01935) 826294

SUFFOLK

Dunwich Heath
Licensed tea-room
Coastguard Cottages,
Dunwich, Saxmundham
IP17 3DJ
Tel: (01728) 648505

Ickworth
Licensed restaurant
Horringer,
Bury St Edmunds
IP29 5QE
Tel: (01284) 735086

Lavenham Guildhall
Unlicensed tea-room
Market Place, Lavenham,
Sudbury CO10 9QZ
Tel: (01787) 247646

STAFFORDSHIRE

Biddulph Grange Garden
Unlicensed tea-room
Stoke on Trent
ST8 7SD
Tel: (01782) 517999

Moseley Old Hall
Licensed tea-room
Fordhouses, Wolverhampton
WV10 7HY
Tel: (01902) 782808

Wightwick Manor
Unlicensed tea-room
Wightwick Bank,
Wolverhampton
WV6 8EE
Tel: (01902) 761108

SUNDERLAND

Souter Lighthouse
Unlicensed tea-room
Coast Road, Whitburn
SR6 7NH
Tel: (0191) 5293161

SURREY

Box Hill
Unlicensed open-air café
The Old Fort, Tadworth,
near Dorking
KT20 7LB
Tel: (01306) 888793

Claremont Landscape Garden
Unlicensed tea-room
Portsmouth Road,
Esher
KT10 9JG
Tel: (01372) 469421

Ham House
Licensed tea-room
The Orangery Tea-Room,
Ham, Richmond
TW10 7RS
Tel: (020) 8940 0735

Morden Hall Park
Licensed restaurant
The Riverside Café,
Morden Hall Road,
Morden
SM4 5JD
Tel: (020) 8687 0881

Polesden Lacey
Licensed restaurant
Great Bookham,
near Dorking
RH5 6BD
Tel: (01372) 456190

Winkworth Arboretum
Unlicensed tea-room
Hascombe Road,
Godalming
GU8 4AD
Tel: (01483) 208265

WALES

Chirk Castle
Licensed tea-room
Chirk LL14 5AF
Tel: (01691) 773279

Erddig
Licensed restaurant
Wrexham LL13 0YT
Tel: (01978) 311919

Penrhyn Castle
Licensed tea-room
Bangor, Gwynedd
LL57 4HN
Tel: (01248) 371381

Plas Newydd
Licensed tea-room
Llanfairpwll, Anglesey
LL61 6DQ
Tel: (01248) 716848

Powis Castle
Licensed restaurant
Welshpool, Powys
SY21 8RF
Tel: (01938) 555499

WARWICKSHIRE

Baddesley Clinton
Licensed restaurant
The Barn Restaurant,
Rising Lane, Knowle,
Solihull B93 0DQ
Tel: (01564) 783010

Charlecote Park
Unlicensed restaurant
The Orangery Restaurant
CV35 9ER
Tel: (01789) 470448

WEST SUSSEX

Nymans Gardens
Licensed restaurant
The Pavilion Restaurant,
Handcross,
near Haywards Heath
RH17 6EB
Tel: (01444) 400161

Petworth House
Licensed restaurant
Petworth GU28 0AE
Tel: (01798) 344975

Standen
Licensed restaurant
The Barn Restaurant,
East Grinstead RH19 4NE
Tel: (01342) 323029

Uppark
Licensed restaurant
South Harting, Petersfield
GU31 5QR
Tel: (01730) 825256

WILTSHIRE

Stourhead
Unlicensed tea-room
Village Hall Tea Rooms,
Stourton, Warminster
BA12 6QD
Tel: (01747) 840161

WORCESTERSHIRE

Hanbury Hall
Unlicensed tea-room
Droitwich WR9 7EA
Tel: (01527) 821214

Snowshill Manor
Restaurant (Applying for license)
Piper's Grove Restaurant,
Broadway WR12 7JU
Tel: (01386) 858685

YORKSHIRE

Beningbrough Hall
Licensed restaurant
Shipton, Beningbrough
YO30 1DD
Tel: (01904) 470513

Brimham Rocks
Unlicensed refreshment kiosk
Summerbridge,
near Harrogate
HG3 4DW
Tel: (01423) 780688

East Riddlesden Hall
Unlicensed tea-room
The National Trust Tea Room,
Bradford Road,
Keighley
BD20 5EL
Tel: (01535) 607075

Fountains Abbey and Studley Royal
Licensed restaurant and tea-room
Ripon
HG4 3DY
Tel: (01765) 601003

Nostell Priory
Licensed tea-room
Doncaster Road,
Nostell,
near Wakefield
WF4 1QE
Tel: (01924) 863892

Nunnington Hall
Unlicensed tea-room
Nunnington
YO62 5UY
Tel: (01439) 748283

Treasurer's House
Licensed tea-room
Minster Yard,
York
YO1 7JL
Tel: (01904) 646757

York Tea-Room
Licensed tea-room
30 Goodramgate,
York
YO1 7LG
Tel: (01904) 659282

Index

abbeys, 46
almonds:
   almond slices, 137
   almond-topped apricot cake, 62
   apricot almond shortcake, 57
   cherry and almond scones, 118
American zucchini cake, 89
Anglesey Abbey, 72
apples:
   apple cinnamon cake, 116-117
   applecake fingers, 72-73
   date and apple slice, 26
   Dolbury cake, 32
   Gloucester apple shortbread, 94
   pratie cake, 139
   spicy apple flan, 76
   Suffolk apple cake, 81
   Sussex apple cake, 63
   Tafferty tart, 115
   Wilfra apple cake, 104
apricots:
   almond-topped apricot cake, 62
   apricot almond shortcake, 57
   apricot sesame slice, 36
   apricot Swiss roll, 22

baking powder, 11
bananas:
   banana and fruit cake, 138
   banana and pineapple cake, 57
   Cornish banana cake, 37
Banbury cakes, 93
bannock, sweet wholemeal, 140
bara brith, 125-126
barm brack, 140
Bateman's, 54-55
Bateman's soda bread, 55
Bath buns, 51
Bedruthan steps, 22
Beningbrough Hall, 95-96
bicarbonate of soda, 11
biscuits, 13
   abbeys, 46
   chocolate digestives, 36
   Cornish fairings, 40-41
   Easter biscuits, 41
   fat rascals, 107
   Grantham gingerbreads, 80

gypsy creams, 134
Linzer biscuits, 106
macaroons, 44
Melbourne wakes cakes, 84
melting moments, 106
orange crisps, 107
peanut and orange cookies,
   45
blackberry tea bread, 44
Blackmore Vale cake, 42
Blickling Hall, 74
boiled date and walnut loaf, 29
boiled whiskey cake, 133
Boodle cake, 64
Box Hill, 56
Box Hill bread pudding, 58
boxty bread, 141
Branscombe Bakery, 23
bread, 17
   Bateman's soda bread, 55
   boxty bread, 141
   buttermilk oaten bread, 141
   herb bread, 88
   organic wholewheat bread, 23-24
   raisin and bran bread, 68
   Ripon Christmas bread, 108
bread pudding, Box Hill, 58
Buckland Abbey, 25
buns:
   Bath buns, 51
   Chelsea buns, 69-70
   hot cross buns, 47
   Pembrokeshire buns, 129
butter, 12
buttermilk, 11
   buttermilk oaten bread, 141

Calke Abbey, 84
Canons Ashby, 85
Canons Ashby coconut cake, 86
caraway seeds:
   Dorothy Wordsworth's favourite
    cake, 120
   Welsh seed cake, 126
carob crunch, 88
carrots:
   carrot and pineapple cake, 100
   carrot cake with lime topping, 65

Castle Drogo, 27
Castle Ward, 133
cheese:
   cheese and celery whirls, 92
   herb bread, 88
   Sue's amazing cheese scones,
    61
   Suffolk rusks, 78
   Welsh cheese and herb scones,
    127
cheesecakes:
   fruit cheesecake, 124
   Yorkshire curd cheesecake,
    99
   Yorkshire curd tart, 101
Chelsea buns, 69-70
cherries:
   cherry and almond scones, 118
   cherry Bakewells, 91
   iced coffee and cherry tea bread,
    100-101
Cheshire souling cakes, 110
Chirk Castle, 123-124
chocolate:
   Canons Ashby coconut cake, 86
   chocolate digestives, 36
   chocolate orange drizzle cake,
    119
   chocolate rum cake, 40
   chocolate truffle cake, 26
   dolce Torinese, 90
   Florentine slice, 34
   Mocha slices, 113
   Petworth pudding, 63
   Sunday-best chocolate cake, 24
   toffee bars, 86
Christmas cake, 50
cider:
   cider loaf, 28
   wholemeal cider cake, 25
Clandon Park, 58
Claremont, 60
Cliveden, 87
coconut:
   Canons Ashby coconut cake,
    86
   Lakeland coconut tart, 117
   wholemeal coconut loaf, 69

coffee:
    Daniel's coffee and Drambuie meringues, 102
    iced coffee and cherry tea bread, 100-101
    Mocha slices, 113
conversion tables, 19
Cornish banana cake, 37
Cornish black cake, 52
Cornish fairings, 40-41
Cornish splits, 37
Cotehele, 29
courgettes:
    American zucchini cake, 89
Cragside, 97-98
cut and come again cake, 104

Daniel's coffee and Drambuie meringues, 102
dates:
    boiled date and walnut loaf, 29
    date and apple slice, 26
    date and cinnamon shortbread, 49
    date and oat slices, 79
Derbyshire spiced Easter fruit bread, 94
Devon flats, 52
digestives, chocolate, 36
Dolbury cake, 32
dolce Torinese, 90
Dorothy Wordsworth's favourite cake, 120
Drambuie:
    Daniel's coffee and Drambuie meringues, 102
dried fruit:
    Florentine slice, 34
    fruit scones, 112
    Moorland tarts, 85
    Paradise slice, 77
    Pembrokeshire buns, 129
    Ripon Christmas bread, 108
    Simone Sekers's fruit parkin, 117
    sly cake, 98-99
    Sue's amazing rock cakes, 61
    sweetmince squares, 135
    see also fruit cakes; tea breads
Dunham Massey, 109-110

East Riddlesden Hall, 99-100
Easter biscuits, 41

Eccles cakes, 122
economy shortbread, 126
eggless scones, 23
eggs, 12
eighteenth-century pepper cake, 120-121
Erddig, 125

fat rascals, 107
fatless tea bread, 46
fats, 12
featherlight wholewheat cake, 121
flaky pastry, 15
flan, spicy apple, 76
flapjack, 60
    ginger, 55
Florence Court, 135
Florentine slice, 34
flour, 11
Fountains Abbey, 101
fruit cakes, 18
    almond-topped apricot cake, 62
    banana and fruit cake, 138
    banana and pineapple cake, 57
    Blackmore Vale cake, 42
    boiled whiskey cake, 133
    Boodle cake, 64
    cider loaf, 28
    Cornish black cake, 52
    cut and come again cake, 104
    Dolbury cake, 32
    giant's boiled fruit cake, 137
    Irish plum cake, 139
    Kentish hop pickers' cake, 66
    mincemeat cake, 76
    Old Peculier fruit cake, 102
    pineapple boiled cake, 136
    plum loaf, 43
    sherry fruit cake, 27
    Simnel cake, 30-31
    Suffolk apple cake, 81
    Sussex apple cake, 63
    traditional Christmas cake, 50
    Welsh lardy cake, 131
    wholemeal cider cake, 25
fruit cheesecake, 124
fruit scones, 112

giant's boiled fruit cake, 137
Giant's Causeway, 136

ginger:
    ginger and treacle scones, 79
    ginger bars, 73
    ginger flapjack, 38
    Grantham gingerbreads, 80
    Grasmere gingerbread, 122
    orange gingerbread, 55-56
    Simone Sekers's fruit parkin, 117
    Welsh honey and ginger cake, 130-1
Gloucester apple shortbread, 94
golden syrup, 12
    Norfolk tart, 80
Grantham gingerbreads, 80
Grasmere gingerbread, 122
gypsy creams, 134

heavy cake, 53
herb bread, 88
Hidcote Manor Garden, 89
honey, 12
    honey tea bread, 34
    Irish honey scones, 142
    seventeenth-century honey cake, 114-115
    Walsingham honey cake, 75
    Welsh honey and ginger cake, 130-131
    Welsh honey bread, 130
hot cross buns, 47
huffkins, Kentish, 70

iced coffee and cherry tea bread, 100-101
Ickworth, 75-76
Irish honey scones, 142
Irish plum cake, 139
Irish potato cakes, 142

Kedleston Hall, 90-91
Kedleston marmalade cake, 91
Kentish hop pickers' cake, 66
Kentish huffkins, 70
Kentish pudding pies, 67
Killerton, 32
Kingston Lacy, 33-34

Lakeland coconut tart, 117
Lancaster lemon tart, 111
Lanhydrock, 35
lard, 12
Lavenham Guildhall, 77

lemon:
  Lancaster lemon tart, 117
  orange and lemon cake, 59
  sticky lemon cake, 28-29
light sponge cake, 124-125
lime topping, carrot cake with, 65
Linzer biscuits, 106
Little Moreton Hall, 112
Longshaw Estate, 92
Longshaw tart, 93

macaroons, 44
Madeira cake, 96
maids of honour, 70
Manchester tart, 111
margarine, 12
marmalade:
  Kedleston marmalade cake, 91
  marmalade cake, 96
marzipan:
  Simnel cake, 30-31
Melbourne wakes cakes, 84
melting moments, 106
meringues, Daniel's coffee and
    Drambuie, 102
mincemeat:
  Dolbury cake, 32
  mincemeat cake, 76
Mocha slices, 113
Montacute House, 38
Moorland tarts, 85
Moseley Old Hall, 113-114
muesli:
  streusal crunchy cake, 119
muffins, Scarborough, 108

Norfolk tart, 80

oats:
  abbeys, 46
  buttermilk oaten bread, 141
  date and oat slices, 79
  flapjack, 60
  ginger flapjack, 38
  Simone Sekers's fruit parkin, 117
oil, 12
Old Peculier fruit cake, 102
orange:
  chocolate orange drizzle cake,
    119
  orange and lemon cake, 59
  orange crisps, 107

orange gingerbread, 55-56
orange tea bread, 114
peanut and orange cookies, 45
organic wholewheat bread, 23-24
oven temperatures, 13

Paradise slice, 77
parkin, Simone Sekers's fruit, 117
pastry, 14
  flaky, 15
  puff, 15
  rich shortcrust, 16
  rough puff, 16
  shortcrust, 16
peanuts:
  Longshaw tart, 93
  peanut and orange cookies, 45
Pembrokeshire buns, 129
Penrhyn Castle, 127
pepper cake, eighteenth-century,
    120-121
Petworth, 62
Petworth pudding, 63
pineapple:
  banana and pineapple cake, 57
  carrot and pineapple cake, 100
  pineapple boiled cake, 136
  pineapple upside-down cake, 39
plum loaf, 43
Polesden Lacey, 64
potatoes:
  boxty bread, 141
  Irish potato cakes, 142
  pratie cake, 139-140
Powis Castle, 128
pratie cake, 139-140
puff pastry, 15

Quarry Bank Mill, 116

raisin and bran bread, 68
raising agents, 11
rich shortcrust pastry, 16
Ripon Christmas bread, 108
rock cakes, Sue's amazing, 61
rolls, sesame, 48
rough puff pastry, 16
Rowallane Garden, 138
Rufford Old Hall, 118
rum:
  chocolate rum cake, 40
rusks, Suffolk, 78

saffron cake, 30
St Michael's Mount, 39
Sally Lunns, 53
sandwich cakes, 18
Scarborough muffins, 108
scones, 18
  cherry and almond scones, 118
  eggless scones, 23
  fruit scones, 112
  ginger and treacle scones, 61
  Irish honey scones, 142
  Sue's amazing cheese scones,
    61
  Welsh cheese and herb scones,
    127
  wholemeal fruit scones, 33
secretary tarts, 65
sesame seeds:
  apricot sesame slice, 36
  sesame rolls, 48
seventeenth-century honey cake,
    114-115
sherry fruit cake, 27
shortbread:
  date and cinnamon shortbread, 49
  economy shortbread, 126
  Gloucester apple shortbread, 94
  wholemeal shortbread, 56
shortcake, apricot almond, 57
shortcrust pastry, 16
Simnel cake, 30-31
Simone Sekers's fruit parkin, 117
singin' hinny, 98
Sissinghurst, 66
sly cake, 98-99
soda bread, Bateman's, 55
sour milk, 11
spice cake, 59
spicy apple flan, 76
sponge cakes, 18
Spread Eagle Inn, 42
Standen, 67-68
sticky lemon cake, 28-29
Stiffkey cakes, 74
streusal crunchy cake, 119
Studley Royal, 101
Sue's amazing cheese scones, 61
Sue's amazing rock cakes, 61
Suffolk apple cake, 81
Suffolk cakes, 81
Suffolk fourses, 82
Suffolk rusks, 78

sugar, 12
Sunday-best chocolate cake, 24
Sussex apple cake, 63
sweet wholemeal bannock, 140
sweetmince squares, 135
Swiss roll, apricot, 22

Tafferty tart, 115
tarts:
    cherry Bakewells, 91
    Kentish pudding pies, 67
    Lakeland coconut tart, 117
    Lancaster lemon tart, 111
    Longshaw tart, 93
    maids of honour, 70
    Manchester tart, 111
    Moorland tarts, 85
    Norfolk tart, 80
    secretary tarts, 65
    Tafferty tart, 115
    treacle tart, 97
    Yorkshire curd cheesecake, 99
    Yorkshire curd tart, 101
tea breads:
    bara brith, 125-126
    barm brack, 140
    blackberry tea bread, 44

    boiled date and walnut loaf, 29
    carrot and pineapple cake, 100
    Derbyshire spiced Easter fruit
      bread, 94
    fatless tea bread, 46
    honey tea bread, 34
    iced coffee and cherry tea bread,
      100-101
    orange tea bread, 114
    saffron cake, 30
    sweet wholemeal bannock, 140
    threshing cake, 130
    Welsh honey bread, 130
    wholemeal coconut loaf, 69
temperatures, oven, 13
threshing cake, 130
tins, preparation, 13
toffee bars, 86
traditional Christmas cake, 50
treacle, 12
    ginger and treacle scones, 79
    treacle tart, 97
Treasurer's House, York, 103
Trelissick, 43
Trerice, 45

upside-down cake, pineapple, 39

The Vyne, 49

Wallington, 105
walnuts:
    boiled date and walnut loaf, 29
    secretary tarts, 65
Walsingham honey cake, 75
Welsh cakes, 129
Welsh cheese and herb scones, 127
Welsh honey and ginger cake,
    130-131
Welsh honey bread, 130
Welsh lardy cake, 131
Welsh seed cake, 126
whiskey cake, boiled, 133
wholemeal cider cake, 25
wholemeal coconut loaf, 69
wholemeal fruit scones, 33
wholemeal shortbread, 56
wholewheat bread, 23-24
Wilfra apple cake, 104
Wimpole Hall, 78-79
Wordsworth House, 120

yeast, 11
Yorkshire curd cheesecake, 99
Yorkshire curd tart, 101